A Beautiful Game

Sven-Göran Eriksson was born and grew up in Sweden. Though a talented footballer, it was in football management that he found rapid success and was headhunted by a string of world-famous European clubs – Göteborg, Benfica, Roma, Lazio – winning many national and international trophies. In 2001, he became England's first foreign manager, reversing years of decline and turning the squad into true World Cup contenders. This was followed by stints managing Manchester City, Mexico, Ivory Coast, Leicester City and in China. In January 2024, it was announced that he had terminal cancer and he passed away in August of that year.

Bengt Berg, born in 1946 in Torsby, is an author, poet and childhood friend of Sven-Göran Eriksson. He has published over 50 books and received numerous prestigious awards for his writing. Between 2021 and 2024, Bengt and Sven-Göran discussed football and the great adventures and mysteries of life over 250 cups of coffee.

A Beautiful Game

Reflections on life and football

SVEN-GÖRAN ERIKSSON
TOGETHER WITH BENGT BERG

Translated by Donald Macqueen

MICHAEL JOSEPH

PENGUIN MICHAEL JOSEPH

UK | USA | Canada | Ireland | Australia
India | New Zealand | South Africa

Penguin Michael Joseph, Penguin Random House UK,
One Embassy Gardens, 8 Viaduct Gardens, London SW11 7BW

penguin.co.uk
global.penguinrandomhouse.com

Penguin
Random House
UK

First published in Sweden as *En Underbar Resa* by Mondial 2024
First published in Great Britain by Penguin Michael Joseph 2024

002

Set in 15.5/18.4pt Garamond MT Pro
Typeset by Jouve (UK), Milton Keynes
Printed and bound in Great Britain by Clays Ltd, Elcograf S.p.A.

The authorized representative in the EEA is Penguin Random House Ireland,
Morrison Chambers, 32 Nassau Street, Dublin D02 YH68

A CIP catalogue record for this book is available from the British Library

HARDBACK ISBN: 978-0-241-73151-2
TRADE PAPERBACK ISBN: 978-0-241-73152-9

greenpenguin.co.uk

MIX
Paper | Supporting
responsible forestry
FSC® C018179

Penguin Random House is committed to a
sustainable future for our business, our readers
and our planet. This book is made from Forest
Stewardship Council® certified paper.

Football

The planet is not dissimilar to a football,
    at any rate
Balls are kicked all over the globe, and
    both are round.

People dribble and shoot, they miss and
    sometimes
It proves to be a goal.
Or a throw-in, maybe a corner.

All over in shantytowns in the Third World
Sprouts the gilt-edged hope,
Inside the dreaming heads of sweating boys
Runs the road; in shabby English suburban flats
The hangover is damped down and life is
    resuscitated by:

MATCH TODAY!

Fraternity emerges, directly contradicting the
    evening papers'
Promised match of hatred, items of faith are
    subordinated,

Skin colour means less than a bad pass,
Great tenderness breaks out, as does violence,
 even war
– anything's possible in the shadow of football,
 on and around
These most-often green rectangles all across
 the world.

Bengt Berg

Contents

Foreword:
Creatures of a Day

'Tomorrow we'll all be a narrative,' wrote the Jewish-American Nobel laureate Isaac Bashevis Singer. But where does the narrative of a human begin? It can be hard to give a single, brief response. We're born into our narrative and involuntarily named its chairperson, the narrator, the actor. The events in this book start with the young, everyday Torsby lad, Sven-Göran Eriksson, who, thanks to his love of football and a growing interest in the game, would assume a new and well-known identity: 'Svennis' on Swedish ground, and 'Mr Eriksson' out in the world.

Everyone who has commuted to and from work, or regularly undertaken the same return trip, knows how repetition can provide space for excursions in the mind, both backwards in time or out and about in the landscape. Suddenly you discover a new house over there at the edge of the woods, even though that house has stood there ever since it was built eighty years ago. The workshop of perceptions, like the wardrobe of memory in the mind, is an institution.

I'm sitting in my white Volvo, following the familiar curves of the road, where hand-painted '*Warning – ELK*' signs appear now and then. When I'm heading back home, I think about what we've talked about, and what it might be about tomorrow when, sometime after nine in the morning, I drive south towards Björkefors, Svennis's house. On the way, I stop at a level-crossing for the diesel train and can then tell whether I'm ten minutes late, or right on time.

Fensbol, my village, is ten kilometres north of the main town in the area, Torsby, and has been the starting point for all these trips to new conversations with Svennis in Edsbjörke, on the eastern shore of Upper Lake Fryken. The drive goes through the villages of Utterbyn, Röbjörkeby, and Oleby and then runs southward, parallel to the railway, past Badabruk, the lovely church village of Lysvik – which is not called 'the gem of Lake Fryken' for nothing – Ivarsbjörke, with its well-preserved depot, and onward to Edsbjörke, where I turn off at the Lappnäs road sign. From there a tree-lined drive leads to the gates, and behind them looms the handsome Björkefors manor house.

——

Svennis and my backgrounds are quite similar, with parents who were ordinary people during our childhood and youth in a rather idyllic Sweden after the end of the Second World War. Early on, from our early teens, it was our shared interest in sports that brought us together. Svennis continued along that road, with well-known success, while I tried to sublimate my broken sports dreams with the challenges that writing can present. If Svennis made his round-the-world journey with the help of a well-pumped football, for me it was the banana peel of poetry that allowed me to visit remote countries, places, and poetry festivals around the planet. He became that world-famous trainer icon who had a reserved seat at international football arenas. My own road was very different, even though my youthful dreams were hewn from the same tree as his. With the help of the golden wings of football he rose above the blue hills of our home to exchange the silence of the forests for another, triumphant, reality. Whereas Svennis came to lead great football teams in front of enormous grandstands, my future would be in one of the loneliest professions, namely that of an author. Nevertheless there are certain similarities in our life stories, with another world ever enticing us, and a home that was always there, offering us security.

Central Torsby, 1950s.

Our contact has been irregular through the years, but always tied to our shared point of departure: Torsby, a town in northern Värmland, right next to Norway. From there, we both sailed out into life and the world, and this book deals with the marvellous journey that Svennis has accomplished through the roughly one hundred conversations we've had since the spring of 2021, during which we've sat with our coffee cups and a grand vista of Upper Lake Fryken and the forest-clad hills to the northwest. Our conversations have ranged widely through time and space, like a spring brook that babbles and sparkles, pauses a while and then rushes on, down to the larger waterways, indeed to the seas of the world.

'People are not where their shoes stand, but rather where their dreams are,' as the Swedish author Ivar Lo-Johansson is reported to have said. The common driving force within both of us has simply been the dream of something more, something larger than the tranquil everyday reality of Torsby as we grew up at the slow-trot pace of the post-war period. So, let's start there and then.

———

In the second half of the 1940s, life in the Swedish countryside still reflected the old self-sufficiency of agrarian society – small scale and robust. And yet in this time of transition, you could sense how the privations and isolation of war had begun to be replaced by an urban, optimistic, and centralised belief in a future of slow but steady improvements, greater prosperity, and material growth. This structural transformation ultimately changed a vibrant countryside into a depopulated rural area.

It was in this social wrinkle that we grew up, Svennis and me and all our peers, who can be seen in school portraits taken in chalk-smelling, calm classrooms. Hyphenated first names like Sven-Göran were extremely common then, and, like certain monosyllabic boys' names such as Bengt, Mats, and Kurt, nowadays serve as virtual certification of being a pensioner.

When you look back to those vigorous and important years of your life, it's easy to grow nostalgic, of course, even to be astounded by the slow progression to a more highly developed society. In particular, there was a natural place for yearning in our young minds, due to the fact that it took a considerable amount of time for us to get what we wanted: new ice-skates, a bicycle, a train trip to Stockholm. The concept of 'recreation' had hardly been invented, much less recreational activities. But we threw ourselves into these changes, embracing every novelty that came along. In those days, you did most things yourself. No matter the season, we were constantly forming new associations or arranging our own Olympics.

Even though I had a two-year head start on Svennis out in the world, our childhood and teenage years provided the same memories and perceptions of the limited realm that was ours back then. However, it was different growing up in the centre of Torsby, as Svennis did, compared with the winding dirt village road where I lived, two kilometres north.

Torsby station, 1950s.

As the central town in a wide-ranging area of northern Värmland, Torsby was perceived as an expansive metropolis. It was on the railway, and it had a large county hospital, which became its largest workplace. Another workplace, more male oriented, was Notnäs Sawmill, which also symbolised the important role played by forestry and timber both in people's gainful employment and in company profits in those days. Buildings that contributed to the urban feeling included the grand district courthouse, the Värmland Bank building, and the beautiful Star cinema, all on the town's main artery, Railway Street. Also within the ambit of local self-sufficiency were a brewery, a dairy, a household store, and other conventional shops.

Parallel to Railway Street ran the town's *La Strada d'amore*, Lort Brook Avenue – or New Plaza Street, its more official name – with bustling life around the bus station and the GDG (Gothenburg–Dalecarlia–Gävle Traffic Administration) newsstand, where Ulla Eriksson, Svennis's mother, worked.

From the railway station the ground slopes down to the water and the pond at Foundry Avenue. Svennis grew up in a two-storey house in what must have been a truly idyllic place in the 1950s. It was close to Holmes School, close to the water, where the salmon queued up to be pulled out, close to the centre of Torsby. Indeed, close to everything necessary.

In the ironmonger's shop window, just in time for the much-anticipated 'Display Sunday' in December, a television set was mounted, a marvel of black-and-white flutter. On the screen, sharp-sighted viewers could make out the contours of ice-hockey players chasing a puck in some remote place. It was magical when that word still meant something: magical!

You could say that television came to the area *before* the picture itself, in the form of the mast atop Blueberry Hill, which was then able to convey that picture very conveniently in time for the Rome Olympics in August and September 1960.

———

As our youthful paths first crossed on a sports ground in northern Värmland, where we tested our mettle in the toughest discipline of athletics, decathlon, we can, for the sake of simplicity, liken the story of this book to a triple jump.

The first step was taken at Björnevi Sports Ground sometime in the transition from the 1950s to the 1960s, with the Rome Olympics serving as an inspiring mirage in a fluttering television set. After that, Svennis threw himself into football, wearing the blue-and-white uniform of Torsby IF. This book tells the story of his continuous quest for the towers and pinnacles of football.

Step number two took place several decades later, at Stadio Olimpico in Rome, when Svennis had his triumphant years with another blue-and-white team, Lazio. We were damned lucky to wind up in the Tribuna d'Onore Sinistra, the grandstand of honour, among the cardinals, the carabinieri, the potentates, and the occasional family with children who had taken their seats on that Sunday. The Italian national team was playing an international all-star team featuring names like Cordoba, Masinga and Batista. American gospel music filled the arena before the black limousine with the bravely waving Pope John Paul II rolled in. What was being celebrated this day was Anno Santo, the Jubilee Year 2000, and the 70,000 people in the stands had been bussed in from different regions and from all points of the Catholic compass around the world. That's when the first thought of a book was born – though not only in my mind, as several biographies of Svennis would be published in the following years.

Svennis had just signed with the England national team, and newspapers in both Italy and the United Kingdom would soon be dripping with ink. He was going to exchange his successful trainer stint with Lazio for an even greater undertaking.

We've now arrived at step number three, into the 2020s, and Svennis has returned to Värmland after diverse guest appearances throughout the world, to Fryken Valley, his football cradle and also the corner of the world where we can share our northern Värmlandian tongue and understand each other, even when we're not speaking at all.

This notion – that our language is grounded in a shared reality that always makes sense, even when it's hard to understand – is at the very core of the narrative. Of course you can think in Värmlandian, and those thoughts might be the solution to a dicey situation, with the following conclusion: It always leads to something!

Once the thought of a book based on our coffee chats was agreed upon, we saw each other about once a week at Svennis's lovely home. Our conversations were recorded on our phones, and have been ongoing, year round, from the winter/spring of 2021. Our two lives can appear to be more convex than parallel, but the two of us have shared that time, albeit in different places and with widely differing activities. And there is poetry in football, although the inverse is probably thornier.

Svennis often uses the concept of 'with your feet on the ground'. To him, unglamourous reality constitutes something basically positive. So our conversations are on a level that an ordinary person somewhat interested in football will understand, even though those conversations sometimes deal with both the meaning of life and the inevitability of death.

Even in the brief time from mid-March 2021 up to the present a lot has happened, both huge and world-shattering events around the planet and in our own existence. War and misery, sickness and death. All while the seasons succeed each other in our Nordic idyll.

In early February 2023, Svennis found out that he was seriously ill and that all his plans needed to be adjusted as a result. Of course, his diagnosis came as a shock, and initially knowledge of it was confined to a highly restricted circle, although in time it burst out as a huge piece of news throughout the football world.

Suddenly, the perspectives of our conversations took on an entirely new dimension, but our meetings have nevertheless persevered.

———

On the day in February 2023 when he gives me the news, it's not autumn and it's not spring, but it should be winter. We're walking along the village road towards Lappnäs, a tiny and silent congregation sharing the gravity of the moment. The waves on the lake are dark and robust, the clouds are laying their carpets of light over the ridges of the hills on the other side. The wind is southerly, but nevertheless chilling. From one week to the next, existence can be turned upside down. Like a kitchen table following an eruption of anger, or a car skating on an icy straight road, quite unexpectedly.

We talk about everyday subjects involving the area that surrounds us, and then a few short phrases about the situation. There's an atmosphere of trust, muted but tender. That I could maybe live in his lake house, as he calls the place where an Afghan family lived for several years. (They still live in Sweden, in Sunne now.) We also establish that our work on the book is to continue, but everything depends on how the illness behaves and can be managed.

> Creatures of a day! What is a man?
> What is he not? A dream of a shadow
> Is our mortal being. But when there comes
>   to men
> A gleam of splendour given of heaven,
> Then rests on them a light of glory
> And blessed are their days.
>   —from *Pythia VIII*, Pindar

This lovely text was written by the Greek poet Pindar in the early fifth century BCE, and it addresses the brevity of life, but also its unique grandeur: we are born, we live, and we die. This is the same for everyone on earth, and it's one of the few things we can be absolutely certain about. Those who harbour religious feelings can imagine a continuation, of course, albeit in another dimension, after death.

Since Svennis was informed of his incurable

disease, he has had further reasons to reflect on his existential situation, and to navigate his thoughts in an entirely new way. And through his level-headed comportment, he has inspired both wonder and admiration among the general public.

We're out walking in the garden. He turns to the north and points across the water. 'Do you see that promontory sticking out as far away as you can see? That's where I'd like to have my memorial when I've left this earthly existence.' He looks at a bench carved out of a block of stone on the lawn. 'Final resting place,' he says with a smile. 'I turn to both the Bible and to the Quran sometimes, but I can't claim to be a believer.' Then he says, almost as a way of completing the picture of his belief in God: 'The Ten Commandments contain some useful morals, rather than beliefs, such as you should honour and respect other people. But to me, nature is the true miracle. The seasons.'

After learning about his disease, Svennis has had to adjust his clock, change his perspective, and find a plausible everyday strategy. Suddenly the final chapter of the book of his own life is approaching, and now, more than ever, he has to meet each day as it comes. Each morning is stunningly new, and the pulse of life is still beating. Life is worth living.

In January 2024 he declares, calm and collected, so

the whole world can hear: 'Everyone understands that I have a disease that's not good. Everyone's guessing that it's cancer, and it is. But I'll be resisting it as long as I can.'

Then he adds: 'But you have to fool your mind. See the positive side of things, don't get bogged down in adversity, because this is the greatest setback, of course, but, rather, do something good with it.'

This is his standard response to the repeated questions as he's interviewed during his royal progress from one European football metropolis to another: Liverpool, Lisbon, Gothenburg, Genoa, Degerfors, and of course Torsby. People's interest in Sven-Göran Eriksson is overwhelming. The reporters seem to find it difficult to take in his undramatic reasoning about the cessation of life and the imminence of death. But this, the notion that there's a point where everything stops for living creatures, can't this be regarded as just as natural as the fact that a person didn't exist before the meeting of an egg and a sperm nine months before it was time to meet the light of day?

First, you don't exist. Then you exist for a time. Then you don't exist.

And isn't it so that the fresh rose's fragrant existence is enticing precisely because it will *not* be resplendent for ever? The rose reaches its perfect blossoming only to dry up and become a lighter form of matter. An artificial rose might look like a genuine rose, and surpass it in terms of the 'length of its life', but the value of the artificial flower is nonetheless lower.

It's the ending, the ceasing, that lends what we previously experienced its great value to us. This could be expressed in simplified terms, with football references: Imagine a match that never ends, that never culminates in a referee's whistle. Just as meaningless as playing 2 x 45 minutes with no ball.

We're all born alone, and we each die our own death. But life we share with each other, with those who are very close by and with everyone else out there. When someone gets an estimate for their death date, tomorrow obviously takes on new meaning. What was previously a given assumes new value in the new situation.

We're all creatures of a day, and the golden radiance that reaches us can come from various senders and imbue our lives with shifting goals and meaning.

Bengt Berg,
Torsby, August 2024

CHAPTER 1

Torsby IF

In Torsby, as in most communities in the Swedish countryside, it was important to stand with both feet on the ground, not to think that you were better or more worthy than anybody else. And preferably those feet should meet the ground via the grass of a football pitch, the running tracks of a sports ground, or ski boots. Because in the Torsby of my childhood, in the 1950s and 1960s, everything centred on sports. At Björnevi Sports Ground, blue-and-white Torsby IF played their home matches, and they still do. To us children, the arena seemed gigantic, with the PA speakers blaring music before matches and at halftime. But football wasn't the only sport. The local high-jump star Kjell-Åke Nilsson practised his diving style in the evenings until darkness fell.

But we also looked out over the larger world of

sports, which came to northern Värmland with the help of radio and, of course, newsstands, like the one where Mum worked, selling magazines like *Rekord-Magasinet*, *Idrottsbladet*, and *All Sport*.

The Eriksson family lived in a flat on Östmark Road. It had one room and a kitchen, home to my dad, Sven, my mum, Ulla, and later my little brother, Lars-Erik, 'Lasse'. I had to sleep on the kitchen sofa. It was crowded, and Mum dreamt about something larger. Dad didn't think we could afford to move, so he and Mum asked my paternal grandparents to

A one-year-old Svennis.

provide a surety for them, so they could borrow money from the bank.

Grandpa and Grandma weren't rich, but they owned forests and land, so they could clearly put up a security. But no, we didn't get any help. Mum held a grudge against them after that. There was never a really good relationship between them. That might also have something to do with the fact that, during the first two years of my life, they didn't know I existed.

I was definitely not planned. Dad worked on the bus between Sunne and Torsby. He sold tickets, and he was eighteen, nineteen years old when I was born. Mum was three years older and lived in Sunne but worked in Torsby. She took that bus every day. And, of course, they took a liking to each other as they travelled the country roads.

Dad had a guilty conscience about not telling his parents when I was born. I don't think they even knew that Mum and Dad were together. During those two years, Mum lived alone in a one-room flat with me. The building had only one toilet, which was shared by five or six families, and there was no shower.

'I was as damned immature as a person can be when I became a father,' says my dad, even today. He was ashamed of this as long as Mum was alive. He never fought with her – I never even heard them grumble about each other. This might have had something to do with the first years of my life.

Even though they didn't get any help, Mum was dead set on moving anyway. She was a strong-willed woman, and she knew that there were cheap plots for sale in Torsby. She seized the opportunity, and they built a house with four rooms and a kitchen. We moved in at Eastertime in 1959, when I was eleven years old. We were hard up – but she had succeeded.

Mum worked in a fabric shop a while and then started at the GDG newsstand, right next to the train station. She worked there for many years. Then, for reasons I've never understood, she became a nurse's assistant and worked primarily nights at the hospital. This was practical, because it was just across the street from our house.

Dad was first a conductor with a bus company that was owned by my paternal grandmother's brother. Then he started driving the bus instead, before he got a job as a truckdriver. His last job was as a factotum at the shopping centre Toria, where he was in charge of the garden and the mail service, among other things.

By then, Mum and Dad lived in a fine house on Herrgårdsviken in Torsby, just before the pond and the rapids, towards Lake Fryken. I was the one who said that they should buy that house, and they did. But they absolutely did not want any financial help.

Mum was all aglow about the house, and they lived there until Dad retired. His boss said that Dad was the best employee they had, but Dad felt he was ready to leave. Then he thought the garden at Herrgårds-viken got to be too much for him to tend.

———

Mum and Dad were very pleased with my interest in football. Mum didn't attend many matches, but when we played at home in Torsby, she came to watch. Dad saw everything. He has never played football, but has always been a tremendous fan. Today he watches more matches on TV than I do – and that's a lot of matches. When I've gone to a match, for example with Karlstad Fotboll, I can barely get back in the car before he calls me to talk about it: 'How was it? They allowed a bloody goal!'

But Mum was very strict about me doing my homework alongside sports. She always got high marks in school, and her teachers told her she should continue her education. They even came to visit her mother and pressed their case about further studies.

I never met my maternal grandfather. Everybody refused to talk about him. He simply disappeared, apparently. My maternal grandmother had to look after four children, so she couldn't afford to have her daughter study more, although eventually the youngest was allowed to become a nurse. Mum had to find a job, after six years of schooling. She never got over this, so she was conscientious about us getting our homework done and pursuing further education. She was determined not to have the same thing happen to her children.

She thought I was a saint. I could do no wrong. Oddly, I was half strictly raised and half spoiled. I felt a great deal of love at home. But I didn't always do my homework, which made Mum angry. Dad didn't care. He had put in his six years of school and hated every day. That was it for him, for ever.

I was generally a good boy, and certainly not a troublemaker in school. But on the other hand I was a young player at Torsby IF, and in those days you learned to drink alcohol on the football team. We won Division 4 and had a shot at a qualifying match in Kristinehamn. After the match, which we won, the club treated us to dinner at the main hotel in Karlstad, and that included both food and beverages. I was sixteen and had no direct experience of alcohol. They had to carry me in at home. My mum didn't speak to me for a week. The next morning there was no breakfast ready for me, and I had to put together a sandwich as best I could. After all, we had food at school.

Dad's reaction was somewhat milder. 'Well, that's just going to make you feel miserable, so next time make sure you don't drink so much,' he said.

I've never heard my dad raise his voice. If he said no to something, and that almost never happened, that was the end of the discussion. Without shouting. We knew – Mum, my brother, and me – that we weren't going to do that. He never sweated the small stuff. Looking at my parents, I believe that my manner is a lot like my dad's. We're similar both in looks and as individuals, although in my professional life I've been socially schooled in a different way than he ever was.

My parents had some good friends, but not many. My mum was a homebody. I don't know why, but when she died, the rest of us were really surprised about my father, who had always been so shy and quiet: overnight he became super-social. Born in 1929, he knows everybody in Torsby. He goes out for a walk every day. And he gets hugs from all the gals between the ages of twenty and ninety.

———

I worked summers as an errand boy, delivering bread for a bakery on a packmoped. The bakery was next to Majwonne Ceramics, and behind that they had

Looking back, what advice would you give yourself as a child? As a teenager? And as a young man?

For me, the football dream never started on the bench. For a long time, it was on the pitch where I wanted to shine. But I never became much of a player myself. So my advice to myself would be: Train as much in football as you can when you are young. For me, it was skiing, ice hockey and other winter activities that dominated a large part of the year. But if you want to succeed in football, you have to train a lot from a young age.

the New Coffee Shop, where I was a bakery apprentice later. At that café, which is a pizzeria today, the jukebox went full blast, and rockers and chicks loved the scene. Back then, there were five coffee shops in Torsby, each with its own customers and its own social function in the area. Next to Hotell Björnidet was Sohl's, a traditional, older-ladies' café, and further up on Kyrkogatan there was Lindström's. That was a watering hole for the budding existentialists sporting long black scarves, students at the new upper-secondary school. Along the main artery, Järnvägsgatan, there was Henricsdal's Café in an old wooden building. They had a fine veranda that was frequented by bus passengers, who might have paid a visit to the doctor or travelled into the centre on an important errand. And then we had the Wiener Café, which was above the Salvation Army.

I got an old lady's moped when I was fifteen, and the world instantly became a bit bigger. The moped wasn't in great shape, but it ran. You had to pump-start it, using the pedals. We were neighbours with the driving-school instructor, Sahlström, who must have seen me struggling with it. He was interested in football, and one day he said to me: 'If Torsby make Division 3, you'll get a driving licence from me.' I took three practice drives, and a few times I drove around Sunne, which had dual lanes past the hot-dog stands. That's where he taught me all the secrets for passing the driving test. And he was right on the money. I never cracked a book of theory, and to this today I haven't learned to read traffic signs.

———

'One, two, three – ready, steady, go! – NOW!'

And I'm still standing there atop the diving tower at Kollsberg, the bathing place on the lake, holding back. I ultimately had to take the stairs back down, because I never dared to jump. There were platforms at three metres and five metres. It felt like I was at the top of the Eiffel Tower. With dark waves below. And acrobatic people among us could climb up the railing on top of the five-metre structure as well. That made it one metre higher. Even people who couldn't swim jumped off, just as dumb as they were fearless.

It was me, Anders 'PeeWee' Persson, and a bunch of friends. PeeWee was a real handful, afraid of nothing. He was absolutely intrepid, unlike myself. He and I both swapped the summer diving tower for ski-jumping in the winter.

Mum never liked that I was a ski-jumper, but one Sunday when I had been jumping for several years, Mum and Dad said they would come and watch us practise at the Brunnsdalsbacken facility. There was a whole gang of us jumping there, and I told PeeWee that my mum and dad were on their way. When they were in place in the spectator area below the lower jump, PeeWee said: 'Out of the way, children. I'm about to show you how to ski-jump!' He gave it all he had, lost control, and landed pretty much on his head. PeeWee was taken to hospital and stayed there for a week with concussion. That was the only jump my parents saw.

I was also active in athletics – decathlon, to be precise. At Björnevi Sports Ground, of course. It was

a practical set-up where us lads could fetch the shot-put shots, javelins and other equipment ourselves from an unlocked shed. The stopwatch shone like a diamond, and from the library we could borrow an instructive book on javelin-throwing technique.

Alongside sports, I also played musical instruments, first the recorder and later the mandolin. Until I got it into my head that I wanted to play the trumpet, because Göte Norlén, who was my dad's age and lived in our building, played it. He played clarinet, saxophone – and trumpet. Göte's mother, Klara Norlén, would send me to buy her two packs of Florida's – cigarettes, that is. She was always smoking, always had a pot of coffee on the stove, and in a corner there was a bottle of aquavit. She would take a sip now and then. And drink coffee. She lived to be as old as the hills.

When Göte came home from work in the summertime, we wanted him to come and play football, so we had to wait for him while he practised for an hour on his instruments. We sat on the steps while he sat on the balcony and played. We weren't especially interested in the musical performance – we just wanted him to come and play football with us. But I was nevertheless inspired to learn the trumpet. You need voluminous lungs and strong lips. I believe it was more because there were so few players than because I was so talented, but, whatever the reason, I got to play at the end-of-term celebration. I wanted to play 'Summer Night on Gotland', but my teacher, Lawrence Lithander – who was from Canada, from a place named Erickson in Manitoba – didn't think it sounded good, so said I would have to play something easier. But I held my ground, saying that that was the song it had to be. But it sounded atrocious.

One day I made up my mind and told Dad that I was going to give up the trumpet. 'I believe you've made the right choice,' was his response. It must have been awful for everyone there at home, where I sat and practised the same songs over and over again. And, considering which way my life in football was heading, I have to admit that my dad was right. I had made the right choice. But I would like to be able to play some instrument today. It seems to add so much spice to life.

CHAPTER 2

Sifhälla / KB Karlskoga / Degerfors

Organised football first entered my life via very local and loosely structured boys' teams with names like Klypa, Valberget, Ljusnan and Åsen. These were neighbourhood teams, with lads from the surrounding blocks. We played seven-on-seven on the gravel pitch near Klypa. I played in the Valberget team, and we often came last in tournaments. We were lousy.

Later, when I was older and playing for Torsby IF, my dream was to make the A-team. That was my life's greatest dream: to reach further – even so far, as the Milan pro Gunnar Nordahl wrote in his book *Guld och gröna planer* ('Gold and Green Pitches'), as beyond the realm of my imagination.

In Torsby, we believed we would become better footballers the more we ran up the hill at

Playing for Division 3 in SK Sifhälla, 1971.

Brunnsdalsbacken. We did it until we puked. 'Good,' said the coach while we stood there sobbing. We never touched a football from November up until the snow began to melt away. There was no such thing as an indoor football pitch. The conditions were such that we were, as football players, in fairly good physical shape, but regarding technique, there was a lot to be desired. On the other hand, these conditions were the same for everyone. Of course, there's a difference if you grow up on Copacabana and play barefoot beach football compared to running up a steep hill all winter. But we did have great stamina. The most glorious moment every year was when we could go out on the grass with a football. Damn, that was really something.

First I was happy just to be part of the gang and practise, but then came the day when I was selected to play on the A-team for the first time. For some reason, the team roster was always on a sheet of A4 paper pinned up on a noticeboard facing the GDG newsstand, towards the railway. There weren't any reserves in those days, so the list consisted of just eleven names.

I used to ride down on my bike the evening before the match and look at that magical noticeboard. Sometimes the roster hadn't been put up yet, so I would glumly ride back home again. But the first time I saw my name on that paper. Wow! WOW! I was proud, happy, and nervous. It was huge!

In the locker room before a match, I felt that I had to go to the bathroom, which was at the far end by one of the short sides. When I excused myself, the team manager, Sune Larsen, said: 'Don't go to the bathroom. You'll run much faster if you haven't pissed.' As a freshman on the team, I had no choice. Just do as they say.

I've thought a lot about this business with the team roster but never figured it out. Why in the world would they post it on a noticeboard right in the middle of Torsby? Why not tell the players in advance, at practice?

No matter how you look at it, there are always just eleven players who play from the start of a match. It's hard to exclude players. It's not something you take lightly as a coach. We work together all week, and match time comes around, and some players have to just sit on the bench, and some don't have a chance to play at all. They have to sit in the stands or stay home when the rest of the gang drives away to play a road game. Then they're out, no longer part of the group. This is tough. If you're suited up and sitting among the reserves, who have a chance of entering the match, then you're one of the gang, you're needed. Otherwise, you're outside of the community, outside the context. Sometimes I tried to explain why I made my roster decisions, and told the players who didn't make the list that if they wanted to know why they were going to be on the bench, they could simply come and ask me. Most often it wasn't a big surprise to the players which of them would start and which would be on the bench.

I was national team manager for England when David Beckham was acquired by Real Madrid. There he was benched by Fabio Capello, and Beckham called me to complain: 'Now I won't be playing this weekend. I don't know why.' I suggested that he go up to Capello and politely ask why he hadn't been

SIFHÄLLA / KB KARLSKOGA / DEGERFORS

selected and if there was something he could do better. A while later Beckham called back.

'All he said was that he's only allowed to play with eleven players.'

That answer was sufficient, Capello thought. That was his way of saying: 'Don't come and question my decision. Shut up.'

In Torsby IF, Sven-Åke Olsson, known as 'Åsen', was our trainer. Maybe he needed more time to think about the team, so he would postpone the final choice until after the last training session before the match. Maybe he thought it was hard to tell players to their face that they hadn't been chosen. Many coaches who have been unsuccessful have had that problem, disappointing someone. That has actually never been a problem for me.

But Åsen had that fire in his stomach, both for ice hockey and for football. He looked after all the young players, made sure everyone played. He was always enthusiastic. I can't recall a single training session or match where he wasn't at everybody's beck and call, ready to help. He contributed so much to the entire community. I sincerely hope he was well compensated.

—

Svennis in the military.

When I finished my compulsory education, through lower secondary school, I did my military service and then took a one-year course in office work before getting a job at the Regional Social Insurance Office. First in Torsby, where I earned 851 kronor a month, then in Karlstad. As I sat there in Karlstad one day, a thought struck me: Am I going to sit here for the rest of my life?

Nearly all of the employees at the insurance office were women. This meant that my path was already cleared, but despite that, I went up to my boss to resign.

'You can't resign. In a year, or two at most, you'll be the boss,' was my boss's reaction.

In those days, women did not become bosses.

Then I got some advice from someone about a year older than me, Bengt Frykman, who later became the head of Radio Värmland. 'Study some more,' he said. I trusted him fully, and I felt motivated. I was also five years older than the others at the upper-secondary school class, so it was a breeze for me. Without any effort, I got the highest marks.

After a year and a half, I wanted to study economics, a subject they didn't teach at Torsby. I moved to Säffle, played in the Division 3 club Sifhälla for nearly two seasons, and attended school in Åmål. I had a hand in the club being relegated to Division 4. But maybe the most important thing was that I met my future wife, Ann Christine, 'Anki'. Her father was the headmaster of Åmål Upper Secondary School.

When I finished secondary school, I became friends with my form-master. We used to get together for a Pilsner or two, and on one occasion he said to me: 'You should attend the College of Physical Education in Stockholm. I think your grades are good enough to get in there.'

So I did. I was accepted at the college – known as GIH – where physical-education teachers and sports leaders were trained; not the football programme in Stockholm, but rather in Örebro, at the 'regular' GIH. If I hadn't been accepted, I'd probably have become a sports journalist.

My dream of devoting myself to football – as a player, that is – was still alive and well, and it truly took off when I moved to Örebro. But even more important was the fact that I met the person who helped me take the first steps towards making my dream a reality. When I moved, I changed clubs from Sifälla to KB Karlskoga, where the trainer happened to be Tord Grip. KB Karlskoga played in the second-highest division, and I contacted him to ask if I could come to a training session. That's how we met.

The circumstances were truly fortuitous that convinced me to go all in for football, because that's what I did when I met Tord, and after that my path was straight. The first time Tord and I met was in the winter, on a lousy, stone-hard gravel pitch. Then I got to play on the B-team for half a year. One day, the day before a match, Tord called to say that Kenny Kinell was injured and Curt Edenvik was ill. I was actually his third choice for right back, but after that match I played regularly for two and a half years.

On the pitch, I was the cleanest football player you've ever seen. I never tackled anybody, even though I played wing back. It could be dirty and muddy, but my shorts would only be wet at most – never dirty. To tell the truth, I was lousy at tackling, but I ran a lot, up and down the pitch, even though I was playing wing back. My perseverance and stamina were my greatest talents as a player. All those runs up and down Brunnsdalsbacken had produced results. I also never missed a single training session, never cut corners. But a technical or tactical wizard I was not.

I started taking a course for trainers, and when Tord was a player-coach, we really got to know each other and started hanging out together. He did things I had never seen before at sessions in Torsby and Sifhälla.

After a while I started thinking more and more about what was good and not so good about our training sessions, wondering why we didn't do this or that instead. When I played with KB Karlskoga, we played an away match against Helsingborg. They had a lightning-fast left-wing player, and when he moved to receive the ball, I went with him. They put the ball behind me, and the outside left took off. I was five metres behind right away. 'Svennis, hang in there, run your ass off!' shouted Imre Móré, the Hungarian coach who had taken over after Tord, from the bench. 'Create some space,' he yelled. The next time I wound up in a similar situation, I didn't get up on the back of the speedy player. I backed off a bit, and he got the ball on his feet instead and shot it twenty metres behind me. Of course, he won that duel too. Football isn't a 100-metre dash, and you can jump the gun. In the locker room at halftime, I said to Imre, 'Tell me what to do – should I get up close or stay back?' He had no advice for me. But I continued: 'There's a centre back guarding him from behind and a libero behind him. How about you tell him to go out behind me a little, so I can get some help?'

It made no difference what I did. I couldn't win running races against this wing. Imre didn't understand this, so I sat there in the locker room in Helsingborg and once again tried to explain it to him. He ultimately said that I was right.

That was my first thought about football not being only a matter of running.

———

During my third year with Karlskoga, Tord called to say that he was going to sign with Degerfors in Division 3.

'I think it would be better if you quit playing and became my assistant coach instead,' he said. I was twenty-seven years old. I don't know what he saw in me, but we did have the same education from GIH.

I accepted the offer without having to think much about it.

Tord was greatly inspired by the Englishmen Bob Houghton and Roy Hodgson. I would sit with him every training day when we started at Degerfors, and we would go through training programmes. It was exciting, but I had to stop playing football, which was a pity. At the same time, I continued to work fulltime as a PE teacher at Aggerud School in Karlskoga, and Anki was also working as a teacher. She had taken her degree, and we purchased a house in Karlskoga.

Tord structured training in a way that, to me, was entirely new. With him, we practised both defence and offence. 'What do the others do when our right back has the ball?' he might ask. Suddenly there were alternatives to the prevailing standard of those days: 'Go get 'em boys!', endurance training, and long 'Hail Mary' passes that were simply sent on their way. Tord could explain things better than anyone. Who should do what, and when should he do it? In what situations? Tord had a summer cottage close to Degerfors and the home arena, Stora Valla, on Lake Möckeln, so I always went there an hour early. And we sat there and planned our sessions, Tord and I. Nowadays we don't talk so much about systems of playing. He said to me last time we got together: 'Svennis, when your passion for football wanes, poetry takes its place.'

25

Tord is in every respect a unique person and football trainer. As I see it, for many years he was absolutely Sweden's best football man. Of course, Tord is who he is, with ants in his pants. He rarely stays in one place for long. So after a year in Degerfors, he took off for Örebro SK.

Well now, that's too bad, I thought, unsure of what would happen with me.

Tord suggested that I should take over as head trainer for Degerfors, but I thought I had too little experience. And many people were sceptical in Degerfors, not least because I came from their rival, Karlskoga. I felt there wasn't one damned soul who would have anything favourable to say about me. But everything was already in place. Tord had made all the arrangements. So I took the helm at Degerfors, probably against the will of half the board. But his approval was all it took.

I was pretty sure that the players had a meeting where they agreed: 'He's a good lad, so let's test him, and see what he can do.' Tord and I are rather similar to each other, at any rate when it comes to managing a collective, a group. Tord is incredibly down to earth.

When I was admitted to Step 4 in the Swedish Football Federation's trainer programme, I was training Degerfors and was the youngest course participant ever to reach that level. At the same time, I had to cancel my wedding, which was planned for 7 July 1977. For some reason, Anki and I were going to get married at the Church of Sweden in Oslo, Norway. I don't know why it was supposed to be in that particular place, but hotel, dinner, and all other arrangements had been made, and they were expecting us. When I got word that I had been accepted to attend the coaching course, I was happy, though I suspected that Anki would not be quite so happy. The course was scheduled to start the day before the wedding and would take two weeks.

It was a disaster. There were tears and phone calls to my future father- and mother-in-law. 'We'll be able to change the date, won't we?' I attempted. But it was worse than I expected. It's not a popular thing to move a wedding, far from it. Anki said, 'I actually should ask you whether you choose me or your damned Step 4 course, but I won't.'

That was maybe the first, but far from the last, time I gave priority to football ahead of other things in life.

I thought about that when Torsby IF had an A-team match in Division 3 recently. They were short a couple of players, and I wondered whether they were injured. I wondered about one player in particular. The answer I got was that his grandmother was celebrating a birthday – or was it his mother-in-law?

'What's the problem then? Can't he play football because his mother-in-law has a birthday?' I just don't get it, but things have changed. If you'd asked me when I was sixteen whether I'd choose my grandma's birthday or a match, I wouldn't have given it a second thought. I could go visit my grandma some other day.

To me, it was self-evident to choose the Step 4 course. That was a must. But Anki and I clearly perceived the situation very differently.

During the year with Tord as head trainer and me as assistant, Degerfors won the series but failed in the qualifier. When I was in charge on my own, I repeated the achievement: we won the series but got knocked out of the qualifier. But in my second year as head trainer, we won both Division 3 – the Western Svealand – and the qualifier, so Degerfors were elevated to Division 2 in the autumn of 1978.

I had been part of winning series titles three years in a row, but that was just the beginning.

CHAPTER 3

IFK Göteborg

One autumn evening in 1978, after the end of the season, I came home from a meeting with the chairman of Degerfors, Yngve Hjärpe. Anki was waiting for me at home. She was excited and told me that IFK Göteborg had called. Were they offering me a job? That seemed improbable: I was thirty years old, and in those days premier division trainers were normally twenty or thirty years older. Maybe it was the junior team that wanted me, I thought.

When I called them back and understood what they were offering, I said immediately: 'I'll be there!' They wondered whether we should talk about my pay first. 'No need,' I said.

IFK Göteborg had trained their radar on me because I knew the previous trainer, Hasse Karlsson, who had now got a seat on the board.

I'd had him as a teacher in my trainer education, and he was one of the examiners for my Step 4 thesis, on how to play 4-4-2. As trainer, Hasse had led IFK Göteborg to sixth place as a new arrival in the All-Swedish premier division, and to third place in 1978. When the club started looking for a new trainer, their quest took them to Scotland and England. They had a lot of meetings, not least with Jan Mak from the Netherlands. He came to have a long career in Sweden anyway, starting with Halmstad BK in 1981.

Finally the chairman of the board, Bertil Westblad, said: 'OK. We've travelled back and forth and here and there, and we're not convinced anybody's a perfect fit. Isn't there some young Swede we can back?' That's when Hasse Karlsson came up with his idea. 'Yes, there is one up in the forests of Värmland. I believe he won Division 3 with Degerfors. He's ambitious and innovative.'

Anki and I moved to Skintebo, a brand-new housing development in Billdal, in southwestern Gothenburg. She got a position as a substitute teacher but was already pregnant, and on 27 May 1970 our son Johan was born.

—

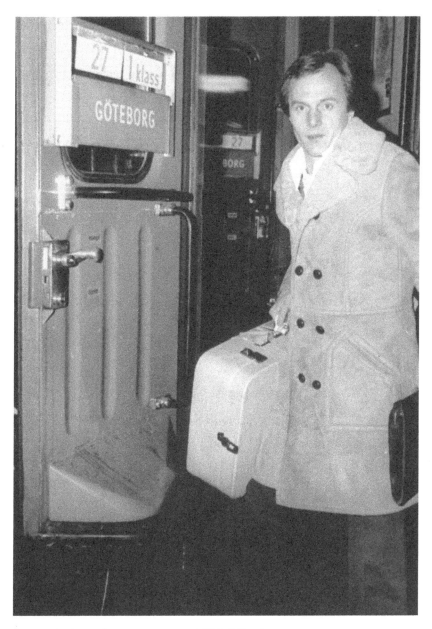
Svennis heads to manage IFK Göteborg, 1979.

At that time I had no relation to IFK (as the club is called), but all of Sweden was following them out of curiosity after they brought in Björn Nordqvist and Ove Kindvall, and Torbjörn Nilsson, who had come back from PSV Eindhoven in the Netherlands. IFK Göteborg was recruiting lots of stars in its return to the Swedish premier division.

When I arrived in Gothenburg, not a single person knew who I was. Not unless they constantly perused the series tables for Division 3. Suddenly I was simply there, with my way of looking at football. It was all about aggressiveness, lots of running and working hard, but it was also about pressing and back-up support, about running routes, overlapping, and playing on open surfaces.

I held my first training session on a cold and windy January evening in 1979. It was on Valhalla's artificial turf, which at that time was always referred to as plastic grass. IFK then featured older stars, like Ralf Edström and Olle Nordin, as well as the new. They had played on the Swedish national team and had been pros abroad – but to me they seemed to have lost their hunger. They had no desire whatsoever to adapt to this unknown Värmlänning's way of playing football.

Reine Almqvist, a former striker who later became a coach, was one of this gang. He didn't want to

Svennis with his son, Johan, at the family's country house in Stenungsund.

play like that. He and I sat in the sauna for an hour after each session. With pen and paper I ultimately managed to convince him, but it took time.

Soon the older guard started to drop off, and they were replaced by a new generation of players who were receptive and eager to learn. There were four Glenns: Strömberg, Hysén, Schiller, and Holm. These young and very different players really wanted to understand what the point of pressing with back-up support was. And 4-4-2.

As a trainer, you have to be in the right place at the right time. If I had arrived in Gothenberg two years earlier, I wouldn't have had a chance of doing what we did.

However, it was easier to convince the players than it was to convince the fans. Many people thought that IFK ought to play the bubbly, offensive game called 'champagne football', and I arrived and offered them the exact opposite of that. It took some time for the supporters to begin to realise that this just might turn out to be something really good.

In my first season with IFK, 1979, we came second in the premier division, just one point behind Halmstads BK. We also won the cup final 6–1 against Åtvidaberg at Råsunda, outside of Stockholm, and knocked out Waterford from Ireland and Panionios from Greece in the Cup Winners' Cup. This meant we met Arsenal in the quarter-final in March the following year. Unfortunately, we lost by all of 5–1 at Highbury in London. I was impressed with Arsenal's ingrained system, by the fact that they all knew what positions they should run to and where they should pass the ball. This made it hard for us to press the ball-holder. I was also impressed with the offensive players' runs and their aggression, not least in front of the goal.

We came third in the Swedish premier division, behind Öster (from Växjö) and Malmö, the team that, with Bob Houghton as trainer, went to the European Cup final that spring.

———

After two years, the IFK Göteborg board came to me and asked: 'What do we need to do to not only get ourselves into Europe, but also go further and survive longer in cup play?'

'Recruit Thomas Wernerson as goalkeeper, the wing back Stig Fredriksson, and the striker Håkan Sandberg. They're super players, and the competition to acquire them is only going to get stiffer,' I answered. We had Torbjörn Nilsson and a young guy, Dan Corneliusson, but we needed to get another first-class striker, and moreover a natural left back. And our Icelandic goalie, Torsteinn Ólafsson, was not up to scratch.

The club did what I asked and acquired three players ahead of the 1981 season. At the time, the club was led by the chairman, Bertil Westblad, a banker and politician in the right-leaning Moderate Party, P-O Johansson, Ralph Öberg, Sven Carlsson, and Hasse Karlsson. The board was so deeply involved that several of them even mortgaged their homes to acquire the three players.

But at first they wondered what the hell they had been doing when they listened to me. The season started with a loss at home to IFK Sundsvall, another loss away against Öster, and a third loss at home against Djurgården (Stockholm). Despite the new players.

The press and supporters were feeling the Eriksson era should already be over. They wanted me out. After the loss to Djurgården, I went to the board and the players and said: 'If you want to fire me, then do it. I still have a job to go back to in Karlskoga.'

They declined to fire me, both the board and the players. They wanted me to keep doing what I do. So I did. But what they actually meant was: 'Keep doing you for a while longer, then we'll see.' I remember the thoughts in my head as I got in my car after the meeting. What might 'a while longer' mean? Was that after the next match, or next month? Doubts started swirling in my head, but I told myself to just keep going. The players didn't want to go back to the old style of playing or change anything else. They themselves had said that they just had to play my game – but play it better. I wasn't willing, or able, to change. I simply wouldn't be able to instruct them as well if we were to change our style of play once again. With 4-4-2 I knew exactly what I wanted.

If we had lost a couple more matches, it would have been impossible *not* to fire me. If I had left then, or been terminated, I can guarantee that my career as a trainer wouldn't have gone anywhere. There was such a ruckus because everyone thought we ought to be winning but started the season with losses. But the whole time I was simply focused on my idea of how we should play football. Everything should be done in a certain way. To me, there could be no alternative, and I'm grateful that they let me continue.

Much later I heard that Glenn Hysén, Glenn Strömberg, Glenn Schiller, Tobjörn Nilsson, Dan Corneliusson and others thought our training sessions were awfully boring. But they put on a good face. A training session might look like this: the goalkeeper would throw to the right back Ruben Svensson. 'Ruben, you now have three options,' I would say.

They all knew the facts – as a player you couldn't do anything other than what we had agreed. Thus, Ruben could play the ball back home to the keeper or to one of the forwards, right on the feet. Or on the surface in front of the other forward, who was running up hill.

That's it.

We practised that for an hour, every single day. The players had to stand in the right positions, and if we lost the ball, we would press whoever took the ball. I stood there gesticulating and shouting instructions. 'You stand there, and you stand there.' I would walk with the players on the pitch to explain. It was a total bore. But also extremely effective.

I did that for two and a half years before all the pieces came together. Then my instructions were no longer needed. We played the same way every match, at home and away. All the players knew exactly what to do in every situation, and they scolded each other if anybody tried to fudge. It was largely a matter of keeping the team as tight as possible. The distance between the centre backs and forwards should be no more than thirty metres, as opposed to fifty metres in the past, in the old way of thinking.

In many countries, such as Italy, Belgium, Germany, Holland, and Spain, what we were doing was completely out of the question. We eliminated man-to-man guarding and playing with a libero behind the line of backs. As far as we were concerned, it was 4-4-2, and you didn't care what opponent you had. As a player, you guarded your zones.

———

Swedish football was divided into two camps for a few years. Bob Houghton, Roy Hodgson, Tord Grip and I were in one camp, so we were at odds with the national team manager, Lars 'Laban' Arnesson and his supporters. Inspired by the German style of playing, he used a libero and wouldn't even talk about zones. Laban had a lot of people on his side.

Tord had been an assistant to Laban's predecessor, Georg 'Åby' Eriksson in 1977–78, and Tord was in charge of tactics and training, not Åby. Åby mostly played the piano and was a good ol' bundle of fun. He had a nose for lining up the right team, and the same can be said for Tommy Svensson, national manager of the team that brought home the World Cup bronze in 1994. That time, too, it was Tord who set up the tactics. But he has never talked about being behind all of that.

He established a school, with many adherents, with his thinking about 4-4-2 and pressing with back-up. First he was my trainer, then my head trainer, and after that I was his assistant for a year. Plus we had the U21 national team, Tord and I, at the same time as I was training IFK Göteborg. Laban was in charge of the national A-team, with rather meagre results, while our U21s won every single match. That was a bit too much for Laban to swallow, so he finally fired Tord and me. We were thinking about football in an entirely new way.

Nowadays just about every team plays the way we were playing, even though it's no longer 4-4-2. The whole idea is for everyone to do their job, to maintain the same distance between the parts of the team at all times, to hold the team together. It was a bit like when the ski-jumper Jan Boklöv started his glider-style jumping. 'God help us!' was the first reaction, but, before long, not a single ski-jumper left the platform with parallel skis. The V-style had come to stay, and Jan Boklöv had changed the sport.

At IFK Göteborg, we had sixteen players in training sessions. That was the total of our outfield players. When we played matches crosswise on the pitch between the penalty zone and the halfway line, the players could only use one or two touches. The tempo was high. It was insane.

I had players who couldn't stand to lose even those matches. Glenn Strömberg cried when he lost, even if the prize was just a drink. If I wanted speed,

I put him up against Conny Karlsson. They were two winning freaks. With time, the players learned to play very fast, with just a few touches. We ran that practice for twenty minutes, at every training session.

Ove Kindvall was sports director at the time, and once he came down to observe our training. It was the day before a match. He came running towards me, calling out in distress when he saw the intensity: 'But Svennis, they have a match tomorrow. You can't have them doing this!' 'Go out and stop them if you can!' was my answer.

After that miserable start with our three new players, we lost only one more match, against Norrköping in late May 1981. And after that we didn't lose any matches for a year, not in any competitive context, neither the UEFA Cup nor in Sweden. We found flow.

The team just got better, not least mentally. Ultimately, we were so good that I didn't need to say anything in the locker room. I did, of course, but they knew exactly what was on my mind. The team developed tremendous self-confidence, and we never made any adjustments. We also had one hell of a streak of luck. For an entire year, we had hardly any injuries. But the margins are small in football. In April 1981 I had been almost thrown out, and thirteen months later we had vanquished all of Europe.

But despite our string of victories, there was

turbulence in the club. The nomination committee decided in December 1981 *not* to renominate Sven Carlsson as treasurer, and Bertil Westblad presented the club with an ultimatum. Unless Carlsson was nominated, Westblad would resign as chairman. All the players signed a petition to prevent the changes, except Torbjörn Nilsson and Ruben Svensson. 'Red Ruben' justified his decision by saying that elections should be run democratically, at the annual meeting.

The club's finances were shaky. At the start of 1982, we had debts amounting to 718,000 kronor, and that deficit swelled during the chaotic spring of 1982, so that IFK Göteborg was in the middle of a financial crisis and tremendous triumphs on the pitch simultaneously.

At the annual meeting one week before the quarter-final in the UEFA Cup against Valencia, the Westblad faction was voted down, and he, Hasse Karlsson, and Ralph Öberg resigned. They recouped their money, but two months later IFK Göteborg were European champions, and they were shut out. The 'Comrades' who had built up the club had been ousted just as they were on the threshold of great riches.

I've always felt sad about the old board's fate. When I heard about their removal, my first reaction was to offer to resign my position. I had a great deal of contact with them, almost daily. When they resigned or were removed, I thought it was awful that they couldn't be there when everything turned around for us.

One evening in February we played Southampton in a training match. Their trainer, Lawrie McMenemy, came into our locker room after the match. 'How much are you asking for Torbjörn Nilsson?' he wondered. Torbjörn had scored two goals and could have scored many more in the match, which ended 4–4 against the team that was then in Division 2. We were going to play Valencia in less than two weeks, and everyone thought we were going to lose. We hadn't played any really big teams before, and it was early in the season – the Swedish premier division hadn't started yet. The first quarter-final was coming, down in Spain, and we had eliminated Dinamo Bukarest, Sturm Graz, from Austria, and Finland's Valkeakosken Haka along the way.

When we arrived in Valencia, we were allowed to use their training facilities free of charge. I guess they felt sorry for us, laughed somewhat condescendingly when they saw what we looked like and how we conducted ourselves. The evening before the match there was to be a banquet for the leaders, but our board had just resigned. On the other hand, the journalist Leif 'Loket' ('the locomotive') Olsson was there, representing the local radio station in Gothenburg.

He had a chance to sit at the banquet, wear a tie and everything. I was not enthusiastic about sitting down at an official dinner the day before the match, but that's the way it had to be.

We talked about what had happened with the board, the players and I. We agreed that whatever we thought about the situation, we had to be professional and concentrate on football.

Then we went out there, a team consisting entirely of amateurs, and played to a draw against a team of professional players. We had hardly played on grass in the spring before that match. It ended 2–2, even though Glenn Schiller had to jump in at short notice because our regular left back, Stig Fredriksson, had a temperature. After that, we sold out at New Ullevi. That's the boost we got in Gothenburg.

Valencia's trainer, Manolo Mestre, had been to look at us several times before, but they really couldn't understand what we had done. They saw us as a team of rustic, brawny players who didn't have very good technical skills. A bunch of odd fellows from the north. But suddenly their players had no time at all with the ball. They weren't used to that. We didn't pay much attention to how our opponents were playing, but focused entirely on our way of playing football. When the final whistle was blown, their supporters gave us a standing ovation.

I then pointed out to the IFK guys that we couldn't get too stuck up, that there was no room for nonchalance in big games. We had to continue to work hard and purposefully – quite simply to play football in our own way. I never talked about us possibly winning the whole cup. To me, it was important to talk about winning the next match. But the players' self-confidence went up like a rocket to the sun.

With that attitude, we beat Valencia 2–0 at home, Kaiserslautern in the semi-final, and faced Hamburg in the final.

After the match in Spain, Manolo Mestre said that Torbjörn Nilsson was the best player he had seen for a long, long time, that he'd like to see him on his own team. Nilsson scored nine goals just in the UEFA Cup during the autumn of 1981 and the spring of 1982. Everything was going his way. But that's not what it was like when he started out. To me, Nilsson was the best player in the world during training sessions. But when it was time for a match, everything fizzled out. This affected him tremendously, and for a long time. In a match, he didn't dare challenge his opponents. His problem was mental. He was afraid to get the ball, afraid he would make a fool of himself, afraid to be kicked in the Achilles tendons. Torbjörn Nilsson, who was 1.90 tall, big and strong.

I talked with Torbjörn after I'd had him for a year.

By that time I had met Willi Railo, the Norwegian sports psychologist. Torbjörn soon began doing what he did in training during matches as well. I would never have been able to make that happen, not with my limited knowledge. I had to turn to a professional. And Torbjörn himself bought into the message. Today he himself travels all over and lectures about mental training.

———

Svennis instructs the players in IFK Göteborg, 1982.

The first match in the finals against Hamburg on 5 May 1982 attracted only 42,058 spectators. Rain was pouring down and the warm, early-summer weather was far away. Hamburg was coached by the Austrian Ernst Happel. They had won the Bundesliga three points ahead of Cologne that spring, and their star shooter, Horst Hrubesch, made 27 goals just in their league. It's also worth bearing in mind that, starting in January 1982, they were unbeaten for 36 matches in a row in the Bundesliga. But they did lose – to us – right in the middle of their league suite.

I talked to the team the day before the match, and I mentioned Hrubesch, of course, maybe for a little too long. Finally, centre back Glenn Hysén said: 'Dammit, Svennis, if he wins a head duel against me and Conny Karlsson, I'll treat you to ten dinners.'

He did not. Horst Hrubesch didn't win a single head duel.

Tord Holmgren cinched it in the wet mud at New Ullevi. He scored in the 87th minute and we won 1–0. Our opponents, with stars like Manfred Kaltz, Felix Magath, and the Danish Lars Bastrup, were nevertheless confident ahead of the return match at Volksparkstadion in Hamburg. They were selling pennants that bragged that HSV had won the 1982 UEFA Cup, but we won 3–0 after Dan Corneliusson,

Torbjörn Nilsson and Stig Fredriksson scored goals in front of 57,000 spectators.

It was a tremendous joy to hear the final whistle sound. It might have been the greatest happiness I've felt my entire career. To have the honour of leading a Swedish team to a European title – that was big. Our feeling after the match was that we had done an unbelievably good job. Of course there was excitement and partying, and the players were allowed to do whatever they wanted. I was able to soak up the victory, but even in that moment I also saw my next destination before me.

———

The following year, Hamburg Sport-Verein won the UEFA Cup. They played our kind of football, with no libero and no man-on-man play.

Today everyone is aggressive in their play. Old stick-in-the-muds like Messi and Ronaldo are the only ones who can't afford to press. They don't pay any attention to defensive play. But they power in goals, both of them, so, as a trainer, how do you deal with them as opponents? Teams try to flip the play as often as possible, to make the opponents run and to gain a little more surface to play on. Manchester

City's play is all about this. Two or three passes, wait, and bam, over to the other side of the pitch.

To replace Bertil Westblad, a bloke named Gunnar Larsson came in as chairman of IFK. His first real act as new chairman was in that 1982 Hamburg final, when he stepped in front of the players, me, and everybody, grabbed the trophy and raised it high in the air – standing in front of everyone. Larsson was a prominent Social Democratic politician in Gothenburg, a municipal commissioner and chairman of the city council for many years. But when he elbowed his way through in Hamburg, I turned my back on him and left the pitch. My thoughts were: I'll be damned if I'm going to stand there with him. So, there aren't any pictures of me with the trophy when we won the UEFA Cup.

I was angry with Gunnar Larsson. He hadn't done anything to harm me, but I regarded his behaviour as more than a little over the top. He hadn't lifted a finger to help us win that trophy, and of course I felt bad about the men on the old board. So I called and talked to them that night. One of them cried, which is perfectly understandable: they had been part of elevating the team. They were the ones who came to me and asked me for a wish-list for new players. When I moved abroad later, to Portugal, Italy, England, they came to visit me. I invited them to come. That was something I could afford, and wanted, to do.

Svennis is celebrated after IFK Göteborg's victory in
The Swedish Cup, May 1982.

When you've struggled with motivation and confidence, what has inspired you to keep going?

When I was young I did not see myself as a leader at all, and becoming the national coach of the English team was something I could not even dream of. But one experience leads to another, and you build confidence thanks to match results that clearly happen. In the beginning, I was nervous about losing my job when I left Degerfors and was supposed to take care of IFK Göteborg with all its star players. I was completely unknown. But when we won the UEFA Cup and proved to Europe that a Swedish amateur team could achieve a minor miracle, it suddenly felt like the world was open. I took that feeling with me for the rest of my career.

Four days after the Hamburg match, we played Öster in the Swedish Cup final. It was at Råsunda (in greater Stockholm), and we won after having turned 1–2 at halftime to 3–2. Another four days later we played a derby against Örgryte. We stood there, the whole team on the pitch, with our opponents a bit behind us, to be honoured before kick-off. Speeches were made, and I had a feeling as I looked at their red-blue side: Today's going to be a flop. They were standing there simmering, while we got lost in all the praise, and then of course lost the match. Sometimes a team's will is more important than anything else in the world of football.

———

After the final in Hamburg, I was with IFK Göteborg for only a month and a half. My contract, which I had signed with Bertil Westblad, stated that I was free to leave the club at any time. But when we won the cup, Gunnar Larsson came to see me and said: 'I've heard rumours that you're on your way out. But you can't leave.'

I explained that my contract said I could, but he wanted to see it, and finally I got Bertil Westblad to call him to explain the situation. 'The clause is there, so don't raise a ruckus. I'd make life hell for you,' Westblad told him. Afterwards Gunnar said that at least he tried.

It made a huge difference to the club's finances that we played to three sold-out stadiums in less than two months. Furthermore, the 'Angels' nabbed gold in the Swedish Championship in the autumn of 1982. I then took Glenn Strömberg with me to Benfica, and that brought in huge sums of money for the blue-and-whites. Torbjörn Nilsson went to Kaiserslautern. The following year they sold Glenn Hysén and Dan Corneliusson. Suddenly IFK Göteborg was the richest club in Sweden by far, and won the UEFA Cup again five years later, with the Värmlänning and former policeman Gunder Bengtsson as trainer, the guy who had been my assistant.

It's truly difficult, not to say impossible, to do today what we did in 1982. Clubs in Sweden can no longer hold on to their best players. The players leave far too early, before they've really found their best form, because player sales are such a big factor in club finances these days, among other things. Swedish teams can clearly, if they're firing on all cylinders, go quite far, as Östersund did a few years ago. That was extremely impressive, but to go all the way and win a major title – that takes a miracle. If today's circumstances had prevailed back in the early 1980s,

IFK wouldn't have won. Torbjörn Nilsson would have been gone much earlier, and Glenn Strömberg and Glenn Hysén as well. But in those days, European clubs were only allowed to have one or two foreign players. This meant that not all talented players disappeared. Moreover, it meant that strikers were the most attractive players, and there were much wilder free-for-alls for them than for wing backs, for example.

—

When I left IFK Göteborg, I missed the players. It was hard to leave them. I felt they were my team, they ran their asses off for me. Exactly what a leader wants.

My last game, we were up in Torsby, playing in something called the Intertoto Cup. It was 26 June, and we won against the Danish team Næstved at Björnevi IP – my old home pitch – 5–0. I said goodbye to all the players in the locker room. It had been a happy time at IFK Göteborg, and I hardly knew what it was like to lose. At the same time, there in Torsby, I felt an emptiness. The players were staying at Torsby Camping at the north end of Lake Fryken, and I drove home in my car. Then they apparently had a wild party.

Inside my head, my thoughts kept swirling around my future: What's going to happen now? How's it going to go? What's my life going to look like?

The next day I travelled to Lisbon.

CHAPTER 4

Benfica

He has been called Sweden's first football agent, and 'the King from Tomelilla'. Börje Lantz, with his ever-present cigar, had come to watch IFK Göteborg's semi-final against Kaiserslautern. I had never met him, but after the match at New Ullevi he wondered whether I would be interested in moving to Portugal and Benfica. 'They've had an eye on you, and they've talked about you, and I can persuade them,' said Börje. He lived in Lisbon and was friends with the Benfica chairman. Then, after the victory against Hamburg, it all lined up, and I signed a contract with Benfica.

Börje Lantz had personality. Anki and I came to socialise with him and his wife Bodil regularly during our time in Portugal. He was a businessman from head to toe – like there was no other way for him to be. One New Year's Eve he told me, with a cigar at the side of his mouth and a whisky glass in his hand, how it all started. He earned his first money at home, in the southern Swedish province of Skåne, by purchasing a large male rabbit named Hasse. He put Hasse in a cardboard box and rode his bike around to various farmers in the area. Börje would pick up the rabbit by the ears and show him off to anybody who wanted to have a look. Then he rented Hasse out for 50 öre an hour, and the rabbit worked hard for him in the farmers' rabbit hutches, meeting female rabbit after female rabbit. After several months, however, Hasse petered out. As Börje put it, he had fucked himself to death. A sad ending, of course, but Börje Lantz loved that story.

For me to take the step of going abroad was not something I had to think about. There was nothing to stop me. It wasn't just another step up the trainer ladder, it was several rungs at once. Maybe not primarily in terms of the quality of the teams, IFK and Benfica, but as a matter of prestige, being out in Europe.

There were a few Swedish journalists who said to me that it was too big and too difficult an assignment for a Torsby lad. They never wrote that, but they nevertheless let me know what they thought about the move. That never bothered me. I wasn't especially nervous when I moved to Portugal. Okay,

Benfica was a major team, but I had a European Championship under my belt, and I understood that they were longing for something new and for major triumphs. I had taken on a bunch of amateurs, like Tord Holmgren, to succeed in Europe. He was a plumber but was nevertheless able to score goals in the UEFA Cup. Or, more correctly, we *together* had achieved something really huge, and everyone believed in the way we played football.

It was like a fairytale going to Benfica, moving to a new country and to a club that is truly famous. They had just finished second in the league, behind their arch-rival Sporting Lisbon, and they were disappointed. With their trainer, Lajos Baróti, they had won the triple in 1980–81, and I arrived after his second, and last, season at a club where only victories count.

Against the wishes of the club, I chose Toni – António José da Conceição Oliveira – as my assistant trainer. He had just retired from play at the time, and the leadership thought he was too inexperienced. Instead, they wanted Francisco Calado, an older former player with experience and who had been faithful to Benfica.

Toni spoke fairly good English, and I liked him immediately when we were introduced. So I asked him right away if he'd like to be my assistant coach. 'Damn right. I certainly would,' he replied instantly.

That was the beginning of a long relationship. Toni is an incredibly fine person. He's loyal, honest, knowledgeable, and philosophical. And he has a sense of humour. If you asked him: 'Toni, would you like a little French white wine?' your answer would be: 'Sure, if you don't have any wine.' It had to be fine old Portuguese wine, otherwise forget about it.

As collaborative partners, Toni and Tord Grip were extremely different. Tord had always tested new things, was always one step ahead of other Swedish trainers. You can't say that about Toni. I had to train him. The way Portugal plays today, that's something they couldn't do at that time. My arrival was a revolution. Everything from pre-season training to tactics.

—

My time with Benfica got off to a flying start. We didn't lose a single match, either in Europe or in the league. We broke record after record. And the philosophy in Portugal at the time was that if the team could just win at home and draw away, they would capture the league title.

The team was rather advanced in age, but I

got everyone on my side. They listened to me and embraced everything I wanted them to do, even if the playing style was entirely new to them. Much later, I found out that the older players had agreed to listen to me and do what I told them, without any protest. Just as the players had done in Degerfors. They wouldn't have reasoned that way if I hadn't scored some big wins in the past.

There were certain other, let's call them 'cultural adjustment', problems. I've always felt it's important to be punctual. In Gothenburg this was never a problem. There I could say to the players: 'Here we are, seventeen people, waiting for ten minutes for one guy to show up.' If they weren't there on time they were fined. It was as simple as that. But now I was in a Latin country, and in Portugal they were more flexible regarding time.

But I was adamant. When the training session was to start at 10 A.M., everybody had to be on the grass at 10 A.M. Not next to the pitch. Otherwise, fines.

During my first few years in Lisbon I lived in Cascais, about twenty kilometres west of the city. That was before there was a motorway out there. We trained next to Estádio da Luz in the northeastern part of the district of Benfica, and I would drive along the coast, with an incredibly beautiful view of the ocean. Lots of people made their way to Lisbon

Svennis in the trophy room of Benfica, 1983.

Is leadership something that is within you, or something that can be taught?

There are courses that try to teach how to be a leader, but as a leader, you must be yourself. You cannot play a role, because to get a group on board you must be genuine, otherwise you will be seen through immediately. Every leader has their style. I have tried to realise mine the best I could by asserting that football not only needs feet and brains, but also that the heart must be involved.

in the morning, so I generally left before 6 A.M. to avoid the worst of the traffic. But one day, when I got on the road a bit later, there was a traffic jam two kilometres from the stadium.

I sat in my Volvo and watched the time go by. There was slight drizzle, and in those days – as opposed to when I simply wore sweats with IFK Göteborg – I sported a suit and always carried a briefcase. Finally, after a long wait, I drove to the verge, slid into a ditch, and parked the car there. I grabbed my briefcase and lightly jogged past the line of cars to get to our training session on time, at 10 A.M. I also ran past many of the players sitting and waiting in their cars.

You should have seen them celebrate! I had to put up with a lot of gibes for having jogged in my suit and because I was so worried about being late for practice. But I did make it on time, while many of the players were late.

I still think punctuality is important, even when we're eating lunch or dinner at home. We decide on a time, and that's the time it will be, not ten minutes before or after.

But the players were not the only ones who had certain bad habits. During my time with Benfica, the rules were that the president, sports director and coaches flew business class, and the players flew economy class. One day the team captain asked why

Svennis with Shéu, 1983.

we flew business but not the players. 'Some day you might grow up to our level,' answered Toni quickly.

We were some sort of upper class in a way I had never experienced back home in Sweden. He said it jokingly, but there was a serious undertone. I never argued with him about that.

———

Early in my time with Benfica, Anki and I were invited to visit Toni's parents somewhere in northern

Portugal. They had a small place in the countryside. It was really cosy, and they were very pleasant people. They weren't poor, but they weren't rich either.

Toni had studied English and French at the University of Coimbra. He was already the pride of the family, but then I came along and made him my assistant trainer for Benfica. The parents sobbed for joy.

They had slaughtered a pig, which they grilled over an open fire. His dad had a huge wine cellar in the basement, and I went with him to see it. The cellar was filled with wines from the 1940s, and boisterous discussions broke out about what wine we should drink. We finally landed on something Portuguese, of course.

Toni functioned as my right-hand man, but we took in Francisco Calado too. He of course accepted all the changes and my way of working. He was easy-going, pleasant. Francisco told me that when Eusébio came as a seventeen-year-old from Mozambique he was already a divinely gifted football player, and he immediately became a huge star. Not only in Portugal, but worldwide. At the 1966 World Cup he was named the world's best football player. But he did have his weaknesses. He liked to drink, and he liked the ladies. Or, rather, he was obsessed with women, and would give them higher priority than the football team. So

Francisco was appointed to keep an eye on Eusébio. They were always together.

I added Eusébio to my team after he had ended his career as a player. By then he had calmed down a bit, but not fully. He was married to Flora Claudina Burheim, who was as lovely as the day. Also from Mozambique, she had been an elite gymnast. But Eusébio was unfaithful, and she knew this – she said she was the most cheated-on woman in all of Portugal.

Eusébio was my goalkeeper trainer, but I never knew whether he would show up in the morning, even though I was one of the people who had persuaded the club to pay him a life-time salary as a kind of club ambassador. He *was* Benfica, and he was largely the reason the club became a major club. But many people saw him as a goof-off, and he came close to being fired several times.

As an active player, Eusébio had had trouble with his knees and often had to play with numbing injections. When Benfica played training matches in the US, Canada, and other places, it's said that the match contracts stipulated that Eusébio had to play. So, he often played while injured. But Eusébio maintained all his life that he was a better football player than Pelé. Eusébio scored the unbelievable total of 733 goals in 745 matches. He was fast, strong, and technically skilled, and his shots were incredibly hard. A story was told about how a striker had been tackled, and there was a discussion about whether this was inside the penalty zone or not. Eusébio didn't care. He simply said: 'Free kick or penalty – it'll be a goal either way.' And that was most often the case. He was very much more of a target player than a passer.

In those days, Portugal was a dictatorship, with António de Oliveira Salazar as prime minister from 1932 to 1968. When I arrived, the older generation talked about how much they missed Salazar. My gardener and his wife yearned for the old days, when grocery prices didn't go up and there was no unemployment. On the other hand, wages stood still compared with the rest of the world. So Eusébio never made a fortune from his football career, even though he signed with Inter. But just before he moved, the Italian Football Federation issued an embargo and closed the league to foreigners, and Eusébio never had a chance to rake in money from abroad either.

Every time I've been to Portugal after leaving Benfica I've met up with Toni, Eusébio, and Humberto Coelho, my team captain at Benfica for the first two years. I kept a house in Portugal for a long time and was there a couple of times a year.

When I was training England many years later,

Benfica faced Arsenal in what was now the Champions League. I went to see the match together with the English press director, Adrian Bevington. He always said he rooted for Portugal – after England, of course – and that his dad was a huge fan of the Portuguese national team. We watched the match together, and I took him out to dinner afterwards. We drove to the same restaurant I've always gone to. First Toni showed up, then Humberto Coelho, and I heard the press director call his dad. 'Dad, Dad! I'm sitting here with Sven and having dinner with Toni and Humberto!' Adrian Bevington's dad ordered him to take pictures, and after a while in came Eusébio. Adrian began to cry, and called his dad again.

———

Benfica won both the league and the cup in my first season with the club, and we also reached the final of the UEFA Cup, which we sadly lost to Anderlecht. The next season also ended with a victory in the Portuguese league, as well as an adventure in the European Cup, which took me, among other places, to Anfield in Liverpool. We lost 1–0 to the red shirts in the quarter-final, hoping to turn it around at home. But we fell short. Kenny Dalglish and Ian Rush and the others were extremely good in that match, and were treated to a goalkeeper bloomer by our Bento. It ended 4–1, and the elimination was hard to take. Both for me and for our supporters.

At the same time, Anki and I began to realise our dreams of living and working in Italy, the country with the world's best football.

CHAPTER 5

Roma

Before I took over Roma, the team were trained by Nils Liedholm, so the Romans faced the peculiar fact of one Swede replacing another on the trainer bench. Liedholm was a living legend in Italian football and took Roma to their first league title in more than forty years when they won the 1982–83 season. Liedholm left some very large shoes for me to fill, and the club that was placed in my hands also had some major baggage to deal with.

On 30 May 1984, Roma played against Liverpool in the European Cup final. In Rome, at Stadio Olimpico. That in itself is remarkable, because it's very rare to play a European Cup final in your home venue. The Swede Erik Fredriksson refereed the match, which ended 1–1 after regulation time. Phil Neal scored Liverpool's goal, and Roberto Pruzzo made Roma's, both coming in the first half in front of close to 70,000 spectators.

It went to overtime and penalty kicks, and there Roma's two stars, Bruno Conti and Francesco Graziani, missed with their shots. Among Liverpool's penalty shooters, only Steve Nicol failed to score. But what was remarkable was that Roma's team captain, Falcão, seemed not to want to attempt a penalty kick. He who was considered probably the world's best midfielder and the best player in the Italian league for many years. And now he seemed suddenly transformed into a deserter, a coward. Falcão blamed it on a stretched calf, and underwent surgery after the season. As team captain you simply have to do your bit. But of course if you, as team captain, take your shot and miss, that's also disastrous. So he had a tough dilemma. It went so far as Roma's owner and president, Dino Viola, being determined to throw Falcão out of the club.

The problem was that Roma had just signed a new and lucrative contract with Falcão, and when I came onto the scene in the summer after the final, there was a major dispute. Dino Viola was adamant: the club would not pay out any money, and Falcão's contract would be ripped up. And that's how it turned out, following negotiations in court. I only had Falcão on my team for a year, and as a football player he was just as incredibly great as his reputation promised. What's more, he was very friendly, and he was a player who did his duty all over the pitch. When Falcão left Roma, a group of players – Italian national team players who had won the gold in the 1982 World Cup – said that they couldn't play without him. They had been playing together for five years, he was their leader on the pitch, and when he played, all the others on the team flourished.

It was a bitter first year with AS Roma, the 1984–85 season. Besides the debacle with Falcão, we weren't performing on the pitch. We were simply playing lousy football. During that first season I regretted my choice of club more than once. I should have stayed with Benfica. That's what the club wanted, and they were prepared to offer me a new contract. And I would have been given a really good contract, because we had played in the UEFA Cup final in my first year and won the league two seasons in a row. Before I signed with Roma I'd also received an offer from Barcelona, but Spanish football was a little iffy in those years, and Italian football was entering a golden era. Serie A had the same status as the English Premier League has today. The greatest players made their way to Italy, where the best salaries were also paid.

But I couldn't get a handle on the old players that

Svennis and Nils Liedholm, 1984.

Nils Liedholm had had before me. They were satiated, and I felt that the first months at IFK Göteborg were being reprised before my eyes, with an old guard that wasn't about to dance to my tune. This included Roberto Pruzzo, Bruno Conti, Francesco Graziani, and the considerably younger Ubaldo Righetti. Plus Roberto Falcão, who had an argument with the leadership of Roma and played only four more games.

I showed up with new ideas and was also stricter as a trainer than my predecessor. Nils Liedholm was seen as a guru in Roma, more experienced than most trainers, and he wasn't as serious about rules and structure as I was. Nils had probably become more Italian than I ever did; I was regarded as a boring Swede. The players came and went pretty much as they pleased, claiming they had been caught up in traffic. There was a lot of friction, with players always arriving late. I refused to put up with that.

My relations with the players were not simplified by the fact that regulations didn't allow me to sit on the bench during matches, because I was a foreigner. The club had told me that this would not be the case when I signed the contract, that I would be allowed to sit on the bench despite the rules. But instead I was given the title of 'technical director', and Roberto Clagluna was the person serving as 'coach' and therefore sat on the bench during matches.

I was the only foreign trainer in Serie A and had to spend the whole first year in the grandstand. It was awful. I could only communicate with the players at halftime. It was like being quarantined. The experience of trying to coach your team from the grandstand was hardly improved by my having to sit with the spectators. Unsurprisingly, the Romans had a great deal to say about some of my decisions during the first year.

In Roma, just as in other clubs in Italy, it was expected that, as head trainer, I would be present in all kinds of social contexts to keep the supporters happy and satisfied throughout the region. For example, in Ostia, outside Rome, 300–400 people might show up at a banquet at the supporter's club. I was supposed to give a speech and respond to questions. This was pleasant at first, but when it started happening every other week, not least when things weren't going so well in our matches, it became a burden. The trainers hated that stuff, but it said in the contract that you had to be there a certain number of times per season. But there was no such thing in England or Portugal, not in the club teams.

At the same time as the dodgy football, and as supporters, press and the leadership were placing demands on me, our whole family was nevertheless able to enjoy the wonderful Italian food and culture. It became a way of life, eating pasta every day, lots of fish and cheese, and drinking excellent wine with our food.

My parents came and visited us, living in Rome for half a year. Dad and Mum had been to Portugal once, but Dad didn't like it. The newspaper *Nya Wermlands-Tidningen* didn't appear in their mailbox every morning, and he didn't speak a word of for-eignese, only Fryksdalian. It was impossible for him to talk to people, and I was away all day, every day. So he wound up just sitting there, making no friends.

It was different in Rome. The house had a huge garden, and there was a gardener who Dad became friends with. Dad helped him, and, despite the language barrier, they found each other, working together in the garden.

We came seventh in the league in this, my first season and were eliminated in the quarter-final in the Cup Winners' Cup against Bayern München. In other words, a disaster. But even though it didn't go well, I never felt that I was questioned by the club. Dino Viola wanted me to stay and supported me. And Dino Viola wasn't just anybody.

Dino had taken over the club in 1979 and was popular among the people in Rome. He had used his ownership of Roma as a political springboard and was also a member of parliament, alongside being president of the club. Dino was incredibly engaged and attended every training session. One day I asked him: 'When a vote comes up in parliament and you're here, how does that work?' He answered that it wasn't a problem at all, because he had a friend on the opposing side who refrained from voting whenever Viola didn't show up. This advanced form of offsetting says something about Italian politics in general, and about Dino Viola in particular.

Dino Viola was a dangerous man. Dangerous and damned smart. Once we were talking to him about his friendship with Giulio Andreotti, who was prime minister of Italy three times, and would also show up at our training sessions occasionally. I asked Dino how long Andreotti had led Italy. 'Since the Second World War, Mr Eriksson,' he answered. He then told me that he would never get on the wrong side of Giulio Andreotti, because this experienced politician was the most powerful man in all of Italy.

I asked why that was the case.

'Well, because when the Second World War ended, Andreotti took secret documents concerning half of the Italian population, the half of the population that counted. So, for the rest of his life, if some opponent got in his way, he simply had to dig into his archive and say: "On this date, you were there and did this and that."'

That's why he had no political enemies. Nobody dared to go against him.

Was that true? Who knows.

———

During my second year, conditions changed for my coaching of Roma. Foreign trainers were now allowed to sit on the bench if they had someone with them who had completed trainer education with the Italian Football Federation. As my assistant trainer, I brought in Angelo Sormani, who had played with the Brazilian club Santos, with Pelé.

Sormani had also played with Nacka Skoglund. To be sure, that Swede was a divinely gifted player, but even when he was at his best, he was slipshod. He went out partying and drinking many times, according to Sormani. Nacka would call him up hungover as hell, early in the morning of a match or training session, and say: 'Come pick me up. You have a car.'

We Swedes have a certain approach to alcohol, but I've never seen a drunk Italian. They have a completely different alcohol culture. If you get drunk, you lose face, and you lose your style, something they don't like in Italy, and not in Portugal either. But they do drink alcohol every day. If you eat dinner with a Portuguese or an Italian, wine will be part of the meal. *Aperativo* will be served before the food, and coffee with brandy – caffé coretto – after dinner.

When I became ill, I laid off alcohol for a long time. But when I talked to my doctor, I asked whether alcohol affects the cancer or the medicine I take. 'No, you can take a drink, no problem,' was the answer. So I drink red wine with food, something I've always liked ever since I moved abroad. It's good for my well-being, and that's something they're extremely focused on in Portugal and Italy – that you should have a dignified and good life as long as you can. I agree wholeheartedly.

———

My second year with Roma went extremely well, but whenever there were major matches at Stadio Olimpico there was tremendous pressure on the seating. From my first arrival, there had been talk of building a new arena. But today they still haven't managed to create a new stadium. They had the land, on the way out to the airport, but no construction ever started.

In the second half of that season I suddenly got some life out of Roberto Pruzzo, who had only scored one goal up to the Christmas break. That was a penalty kick. After that, he made eighteen more. We were far behind in the standings for a while, but we worked our way up towards the top.

In the second-to-last match, we were playing against Lecce at home. They had already been relegated from the series, and winning would have been a mere formality for us. With two matches left in the season, we had the same number of points as Juventus, but our goal difference was better. The mayor of Rome was there and took a lap of honour with Dino Viola – even before the match.

Juventus were playing Milan in a tough home match. It was scoreless at the half at the same time as our match started. Graziani scored early, and we had the match under control. But suddenly our players stopped playing, and Lecce's Alberto Di Chiara was there with a header. 1–1. Before halftime, Juan Barbas made it 2–1 on a penalty.

I was furious in the locker room, that it looked so nonchalant out there when the match meant so much. Were we going to throw away a series championship in that stupid way? There was no point in talking tactics. I just had to get them going again. 'What the hell are you doing?' I yelled. I scolded them and asked them whether they were asleep, whether they were even aware that we would win the series if we won this match.

One of the players said, 'Take it easy, Mr Eriksson. That was just the first half. Now we are going to roll them over.'

The second half was a play against the other goal but Roma didn't succeed to score and didn't win the title.

The authorities started an investigation but in

the end nobody was convicted for match-fixing. Having players on the team that might be willing to cheat on the pitch to make money? That was a miserable feeling, and even though I had two years left on my contract, I considered sending in a resignation letter.

I was never a suspect, but I was deposed by the court. They asked what happened in the first half and during the break. All I could say was that I didn't know, that I couldn't understand it. All I knew was that we simply quit playing. The legal process led nowhere, as is so often the case in Italy.

I spent many days wondering what to do. But we won Coppa Italia at the end of the season, so that was some consolation. The two matches against Sampdoria were played on 7 and 14 June. We lost the away match 2–1 and then won the home match 2–0. At that time half of our players were in Mexico, playing in the World Cup. But we played fantastic football in those Coppa matches, with young players like Stefano Desideri and Sandro Tovalieri. Many Roma supporters of that 1985–86 season remember it as the best football they've ever seen.

I really liked Rome, and all of my life in Italy. But I was angry and disappointed. I had many conversations with Dino Viola's son, Riccardo, who was our neighbour, and we became close friends and played tennis with each other. In the end, I decided to plough onward.

———

During my third year – the 1986–87 season – I encountered more and more problems, slowly but surely, with Boniek and some of the other older players who Dino Viola didn't want to sell. We argued virtually all the time, behind the scenes, even though we were achieving good results. If I sat one of the stars on the bench, all hell broke loose.

But it was also a rough time in Anki and my private lives. On 2 January 1987, our daughter Lina was born in Karlstad. It was wonderful to be new parents again, but it was also a source of concern, because Lina had a congenital heart problem. The situation was taxing for us, for the whole family.

When the season was approaching the end, around Easter, Dino visited us in our flat. We lived in a large villa that he owned on Via Aurelia. His son Riccardo and his daughter lived there, too. And we were now a family of four. Dino refused to live in the villa himself. When he and his family had moved there many years earlier there had been a burglary, so he left the house, superstitious as he was. But he did

Svennis coaching AS Roma, 1986.

How important should the opinions of others be in determining your sense of self, your choices, and actions?

I haven't spent much time thinking about what others think. But at the same time, I don't think I have many enemies in this life. It's important to self-examine, to take responsibility for your actions, and to navigate by your own compass. Have I done something really stupid? Have I hurt someone? You need to understand these things yourself.

dare to celebrate Easter there. When we were ready for a tête-à-tête, I screwed up my courage and told him that it was all becoming too much: 'I know we have a year left on the contract. But I want to get rid of Conti, Pruzzo, Graziani, and Boniek. Otherwise, I'm leaving.'

Dino said that the Italians would be no problem. He realised they were done himself. But Boniek was someone he couldn't sell. Two days later he came to lay it all out to me. It was impossible. He had acquired Boniek from the Juventus family, the Agnellis. The contract was both expensive and lengthy. Dino Viola asked me one more time: 'You can stay, can't you?'

But I'd had enough. If Boniek stayed, I was gone.

—

Around the same time, a certain Silvio Berlusconi had strengthened his grip on Milan. When he purchased the club in 1986, Nils Liedholm was training the team with the classic red-and-black-striped shirts, but the legendary Milan and Roma coach was fired in 1987. At the same time I was contacted by Berlusconi. I was picked up late in the evening by a car with blacked-out windows, and driven to Berlusconi's house, an old church right in the middle of Rome.

'People think I'm going to make Milan Italy's best club team,' Berlusconi said. 'That's not true. I'm going to make Milan the world's best football team. It's happening tomorrow. I have money, I have TV channels and newspapers behind me. So, I can do things my way,' he explained.

But since I was still under contract with Roma, nothing came of it. Instead, he took Arrigo Sacchi, who went on to be extremely successful. Milan acquired the Dutchmen Ruud Gullit, Frank Rijkaard, and Marco van Basten, the world's best players. Sacchi got his team to play zone, and he got the world's best footballers to play 4-4-2. Playing against Milan, it was simply impossible to set up a shot at their goal. They were that aggressive and that skilled.

Arrigo Sacchi was the kind of trainer who demanded that everyone around him should give their all. Everything had to be perfect. He yelled at them for the entire training session. Finally, when the players simply couldn't listen to him anymore, he would grab a megaphone and run along the sideline, shouting.

Ruud Gullit wanted to leave Milan partly because he wasn't on good terms with Sacchi.

He also once told me that while it's true that Milan won the league three times in five years with Sacchi as

87

trainer, he thought that if they hadn't had him, they would have won it every year.

———

With two matches remaining at Roma, I resigned after our loss to Milan, away, on 4 May. The situation was untenable.

I was unemployed but didn't think about the future very much. Lina and her heart problem were more important than football. A few weeks later she was operated on at Östra Hospital in Gothenburg. That day was both horrible and fantastic. Everything went well, but it was a complicated operation, and we felt totally helpless while the team of surgeons did their work.

The feeling afterwards was like getting our lives back.

CHAPTER 6

Fiorentina / Benfica

When Lina had recovered from her operation, I signed with the Florence club Fiorentina. My first acquisition was Glenn Hysén, for 11 million kronor. He was back with IFK Göteborg after a not-so-successful pro career with PSV Eindhoven, and had been a giant when the blue-and-whites nabbed the UEFA Cup for the second time, in the spring of 1987.

I never really liked coaching Fiorentina. The team had no ambition, and that's just not me. It was the first team I coached that didn't have the right will, the drive to win. The club hadn't invested enough money and seemed satisfied with finishing fifth or sixth in the standings. That at least made them eligible to play in Europe. What's more, it proved to be harder than expected to get the players to adjust to the new zone system. Not least, Glenn

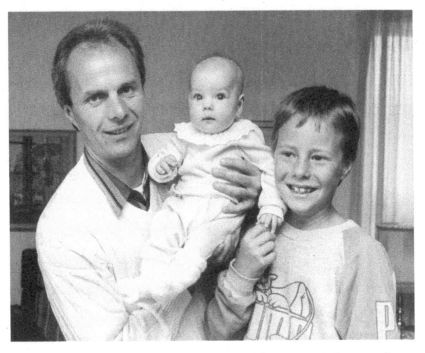

Svennis with his daughter, Lina, and his son, Johan, 1987.

Hysén's centre back colleague, Celeste Pin, found it difficult. He seemed to have completely lost his bearings.

———

One day when I was sitting in my office in Florence during my second year, Roberto Pruzzo, the striker I'd had such a hard time with in Rome, knocked on my door. He was there alone, without an agent. He came to me and said: 'Eriksson, can I sign a contract? I come free of charge. Roma threw me out.' I responded that I was not interested in his services, but he persisted, promising that I would see a different Pruzzo if I just gave him a chance. I finally gave in. He got a paltry salary, but he did fulfil his promise. And he was magical. At our training sessions, he ran around helping the younger players, never complaining. With Roma he never gave a damn about anything. He didn't play much that season, but he was one of the eleven players starting in the play-off match that led to a spot in the UEFA Cup.

And of course we were playing Roma, on neutral ground. It was 30 June 1989, in Perugia. When there was ten minutes remaining, a young Roberto Baggio was dribbling along the sideline. He made fifteen goals that season, and went on to play for Juventus, a club no one can accuse of lacking ambition. Baggio shot a cross, and it was met by a speeding Pruzzo, who headed it into the net. That was his last goal in his last match before he put his boots on the shelf for good.

After the match Dino Viola came up to me. 'Eriksson, I know I made a mistake. I shouldn't have allowed Eriksson to leave. Eriksson was right about Boniek, Conti, and Pruzzo. The end had come.' He congratulated me, but then said he'd never forgive me for Pruzzo scoring the goal that eliminated Roma.

———

Only once, during my years as a trainer of a club team, was I really exposed to the impact of money and politics in sport. That team was Fiorentina. The sports director, Nardino Previdi, came into my office after a training session. We were about to play one of the major teams in Serie A the next day, and he said: 'Excuse me, I know Eriksson is not going to like this, but tomorrow a draw will be just fine.'

'What do you mean by that?' I said, and he responded with something vague like: 'Well, if you wanted to . . .'

I stressed that I hadn't been a party to this conversation.

We won the match. That was the only time I'd been asked to step across the line to the wrong side of the law. It was also the only time anyone had tried to interfere with my choices for the starting roster.

———

Svennis meeting fans in Florence, 1988.

With Fiorentina I also made the acquaintance of the greatest and best player I've met as a trainer: Diego Maradona, of course. I met him as an opponent with both Roma and Fiorentina, and he's the player who left the greatest imprint in my memory. He was so damned good. He wasn't tall, but he was strong. He was never a big success with Barcelona, but when he went to Napoli, everything came together.

We played Napoli one Wednesday, away, in the cup and then we had them again on Sunday in the league, also in Naples. In the cup match both Maradona and the rest of Napoli played with no interest or motivation. Maradona spent most of his time just walking around the pitch. The league match was the important one. We won the cup match 3–2 and were happy and pleased with ourselves. That's when Maradona came over to me and tapped me on the shoulder: 'Mister, congratulations! But on Sunday you'll hear a different tune!' he said. And that's what happened. I've never seen any football as good as the kind he displayed that day. My left back, Stefano Carobbi, came over to me by the bench after half an hour. 'Mister, what shall I do?' 'I really have no idea, but if you can, kick him in the legs,' was my only advice.

The Argentinian turned us inside out. He simply did whatever he wanted with us. We lost 4–0, and nobody got the ball away from Maradona. Among other things, he made an assist when Napoli had a corner. Of course, I had told my players that if Maradona was turned the wrong way, not to let him turn with the ball. Set yourself up for a free kick or bump him, I'd said. Just don't let him turn forward. So they place the corner short, and our players are right on top of Maradona, who takes the ball and lifts it up and does a bicycle kick that is a bullet pass towards the far post, where a Napoli player appears and heads the ball into the net.

After his years with Napoli, things unfortunately went downhill for Maradona. He was so well trained, so damn good, but then he got sucked into a drug circus that ultimately did him in. He should have had a longer football career and a longer life in general. But I got to know him a bit during his finest years, when he was with Napoli. He was brilliant then. He had a sense of humour and a glint in his eye. He was happy and pleasant. Then I met him many years later when for a brief period I was sports director at the Dubai club Al-Nasr. Diego Maradona had just finished working as the trainer with another club in Dubai, Al Wasl. He had been fired. They didn't actually want to fire him, but Mohammed bin Rashid Al Maktoum and his family run just about everything in the United Arab Republic, and wanted Maradona to be ambassador-general for all sports in the country instead of a team trainer. He had that role for a few years, and we met on a couple of occasions at banquets. Once we delivered a speech together, he and I. It was a tragic sight. He looked like a ball, and you could see immediately how miserable his health was. He forgot things, got confused. I told him that I was going to move to China the week after we met. When he finally grasped that I was leaving, he said he wanted to come with me. But that wasn't possible.

———

In my previous clubs, people were cranky and irritable if we lost a match. With Fiorentina nobody cared, so when I had an opportunity to return to Benfica, I seized it. And that was lucky for me. I don't know whether I would call it a relief to come back to Benfica and Portugal after my years in Italy, but I did appreciate being back with a club where the only thing that counted was winning.

I had spent two years with Benfica the first time around, and then I was with Roma and Fiorentina for a total of five years. In 1989, João Santos had come in as the new president of Benfica, and he determined that one of his first changes would be to entice me back. The timing was also on our side, because my contract with Fiorentina was expiring.

When I had the conversation with Benfica, there was only one problem: Toni, my old friend, was head trainer, and I had no wish to take his job away from him. I asked them to get back to me the next day, and I immediately called Toni. The team had been experiencing ups and downs, and I asked him if he was going to stay on as head coach. He didn't really know, but believed he might not be able to keep the position, regardless. Then I told him about the offer.

'If you're still going to be the main guy, I'll stay in Italy, but if you get fired, I'll come and take the job. Would you like to be my assistant?' I asked.

Toni said he would find out what the plan was, and he called me back after a while.

'Please come. I'll be your assistant,' he said.

———

During my second sojourn in Benfica, between 1989 and 1992, we reached the final, in 1990, of what was then called the European Cup. In the semi-final we played Olympique de Marseille, which was then owned by the politician and businessman Bernard Tapie. He was a playboy and very rich – he bought Adidas just a few months later. We lost the first match away, 2–1. Two weeks later we had the home match, with both Jonas Thern and Mats Magnusson on the team, in front of 120,000 spectators at Estádio da Luz.

In the 83rd minute we had a corner, and Vata, a lad from Angola, scored a goal after a head pass found its way to him. None of us on the bench saw what had happened in the muddle in the penalty zone. Nor were there so many cameras in those days. But some Marseille players protested wildly and that turned into more. They grew angrier and angrier with every minute. The match ended, and we won 1–0 and went on to the final under the away-goal rule.

I went into the locker room to find Vata.

'That goal you scored, how did you do it?' I asked.

'Do I have to tell you?' he wondered.

I explained to him that he didn't have to, not to anyone. But I wanted to know what went on. He stood up and said: 'The ball came, so I hit it in with my arm.'

At the press conference afterwards, Bernard Tapie came in and shouted that this was cheating, that the match had been fixed and they were going to lodge a complaint. It was quite a ruckus. He screamed: 'You're not the ones who should go to the final. That should be us!' Marseille had been playing for 0–0 the whole second half. They merely defended themselves. I don't think we created anything more than that corner.

At the press conference I said that I had no idea what had happened or not happened. It was a real mess, and we hadn't seen any TV video either. Today it would immediately have been shown to be a handball.

Three years later, in 1993, Olympique de Marseille

won the tournament that had by then changed its name to the Champions League, but it turned out that six days earlier Bernard Tapie himself had bribed players in the French league, at Valenciennes. The victory in that match gave Marseille the league win, and then it was time for the Champions League final against Milan.

Marseille was stripped of its league title but was allowed to keep the Champions League trophy and title. Bernard Tapie, who had been so furious at that press conference in Lisbon, was sentenced to two years in prison but was released after six months.

In 1990, just like Marseille three years later, we faced Milan in the final. They had a fantastic team, with players like Ruud Gullit, Marco van Basten, Frank Rijkaard, Franco Baresi and Carlo Ancelotti. And Paolo Maldini. We lost 1–0 at Praterstadion in Vienna. Frank Rijkaard scored the only goal.

Milan was the world's best club team for many, many years. Our defensive play was excellent in that match, but we had a hard time creating chances for our players. Mats Magnusson played at the top for us, and he could have played for about three weeks without ever getting past Baresi and Maldini. It was impossible. 'Masse' was simply too slow.

—

In the summer of 1991, Fabio Capello took over at Milan. As a great former player, he worked as an expert commentator on Berlusconi's TV channels and was close to him, and they had already reached an agreement the year before. 'I'll give you one year,' Berlusconi had told him. 'Travel all over the world, if you want, and observe trainers. All expenses paid. After a year, you'll get Milan.'

It was Capello's first job as a trainer. In his world travels he stopped in Lisbon when I was coaching Benfica and stayed for a week. We had lunch together one day, and I thought he was maybe going to ask me some questions at least, but he simply told me how things were going to be.

He got to take over Milan, just as Berlusconi had promised him. Milan was the world's best football team, and that's where Capello started his career as a trainer.

Fabio Capello is not an elegant diplomat. He's bam, bam! Thank you, ma'am. He has always been a person who would walk over corpses if necessary. But he has been successful, even though his time as manager for England was not exactly impressive. On the other hand, I can personally attest that that is not an easy job.

Capello was a very good coach; tough – but won an impressive number of titles. You can't take that away from him.

In my opinion he had a very tough coaching style, which was different from my style of leadership. Capello seemed to know everything about everything – not only restricted to football. Once, we were sitting at a meeting of coaches, some experienced gents. It was me, Carlo Ancelotti, Marcello Lippi, and Capello. Lippi got down to some personal matters and intimated that a divorce was just around the corner at home. He said it jokingly, adding that he had developed a penchant for diving on his holidays. His wife, on the other hand, wasn't interested in either football or diving. Lippi told us he was still a beginner and had reached a depth of 25 metres. That was Capello's cue: he had dived to a depth of 125 metres.

———

In my final season in Lisbon and Benfica, the team and I faced a great deal of criticism. Porto won the league title, we were eliminated in group play in the Champions League, and Portuguese sports journalists felt, quite correctly in my opinion, we were playing ineffective football, where we didn't create any chances and didn't score goals.

At the same time, I received a call from my old home country, Italy.

CHAPTER 7

Sampdoria

Paolo Mantovani contacted me while I was still under contract with Benfica. He arranged a private plane for me, and we met at Loew's Hotel in Monte Carlo over lunch. He brought along his team's two stars, Gianluca Vialli and Roberto Mancini, who had been telling him that Sampdoria needed me on the coaches' bench. The job was mine, if I wanted it.

The next step was the money discussion. Paolo Mantovani went to find a napkin. We remained seated at the table where we had eaten. He wrote down a figure that represented what Sampdoria's former trainer, Vujadin Boškov, had been paid. 'Wow, wow!' I said when I saw the figure, but Mantovani thought he discerned some disappointment in my reply. So he turned the napkin over and wrote a larger sum.

'Now?'

'Yes, yes, yes,' I said.

He was special, Paolo Mantovani. He had the ability to create one great team, or rather one big happy family, around Sampdoria.

A few months later, at the start of the series, there was a break for the national team, and we had Saturday, Sunday and Monday off. He called me and wondered if I had any plans for the weekend. When I said we didn't, Mantovani said: 'Go to Monte Carlo. Go into Loew's.' I did as he said and introduced myself at the reception desk. I was directed to a suite, and when we headed home on Monday morning, everything had been paid for. He had a big heart, Mantovani. And a big, spacious wallet.

Paolo Mantovani actually grew up in Rome and was a Lazio supporter, but when he moved to Genoa around the age of twenty-five to take a job he'd been offered by the oil company Camli Petroli, he became a Genoa supporter. That love affair ended rather brusquely, however, when the club sold its huge star, Gigi Meroni, against the wishes of the fans.

When Mantovani came to Sampdoria in 1973, he devoted three years to working two jobs. On the one hand he was the club's press secretary, and on the other he was running his own company, Pontoil. The company was thriving, not least during the 1979 world energy crisis. It was probably the only one to transport oil from the Arab world to Europe during this period. That's when he bought Sampdoria.

———

During my many years with Sampdoria, I was called *Il bello perdente*, the Beautiful Loser. We played good football, fine football, but we didn't win. Sampdoria, alongside Genoa, is one of the two major teams in the port city of Genoa, and where I spent five seasons, 1992–1997. We finished second in the league once and won the cup once. I thought that was fairly good for a team that acquired cheap and sold dear.

The great Ruud Gullit was declared the world's best football player in both 1987 and 1989 and played for me at Sampdoria in the 1993–94 season. He was outstanding, playing 31 matches and scoring 16 goals. Then he returned to Milan for a season before coming back to Sampdoria for another stay. At Milan he had had a major spat with Fabio Capello, and Gullit's wife called me to ask if I could make room for her husband. I did, but that was a huge mistake. During his second round with us, he was completely different. The Ruud I had first been acquainted with was happy and positive. Now he was going to show Capello and the whole world just

How have you learned to receive the opinions of others with equanimity?

I never cared about reading about myself in the newspapers because that would have driven me crazy. My advice is: Don't care about what others think, keep moving forward, you have a job to do. Of course you want to be liked, yes, even loved when you are responsible for a national team. But football love can come and go just as quickly . . .

Svennis as Sampdoria coach, celebrating with his players after their 6–1 victory against Ancona in the second leg of the Coppa Italia final in Genoa, April 1994.

how good he still was. He scored a fantastic goal against Milan, like Ralf Edström's goal against West Germany in the 1974 World Cup, right up in the corner of the net. It felt like he had squeezed all his hatred of Fabio Capello into that shot, that was the force it had.

But when Ruud came back to Sampdoria, he didn't seem motivated to play. That's not where he wanted to be. He wanted to be part of a major club, and indeed he was sold to Chelsea after little more than six months. He soon became a player-coach there.

The goalkeeper Walter Zenga also came to Sampdoria. His career was in decline, after many years with Inter and the national team. At that time, my son Johan wanted to become a goalkeeper, and he practised for a while with Zenga. They devoted a lot of time to landing technique, as I recall – Johan was constantly sore. But he didn't become a goalkeeper; Johan became a football agent instead.

Another player I had in Sampdoria was Alberico Evani. He played with Milan for many years and had both Capello and Sacchi as coaches. Evani and I spoke about Fabio Capello once. He described Capello as a good trainer but also said he was impossible as a human being.

But the role of the trainer is very different today.

In those days, virtually all of the responsibility rested on the shoulders of the head trainer. He had to apply all of his experience and intuition to everything he did. Today most trainers have an analyst, or whatever you choose to call them. They sit in the grandstand while the match is videotaped, and just in time for the break, the head coach can get information: what looked fine, what didn't work.

The tactics of a match are best observed from the short side. There you can see how both teams have set themselves up and move around. Sitting on a short side, you can really see, for example, what passing options a right back has. He can send off a long, hard, opening diagonal pass to the left wing, who has already started to run – spurting. When the ball lands, far into the opponents' half of the pitch, the left wing has to be there. For this to work, the ball must be perfectly shot in terms of precision and velocity. It's a matter of instinctively figuring out how quickly the left wing can cover that ground.

But it requires timing, it requires genius, a feeling for the game far beyond that of a normal football player, to be able to send off passes that truly open up the play. And at Sampdoria, I met the greatest genius of them all: Roberto Mancini.

He was that kind of player. But he was also a per-fectionist, and he's the same as a coach. He placed and places demands on himself and his players. With Sampdoria he scolded everybody about everything, but he treated the entire team, both players and leaders, to dinner at the same fine fish restaurant every Friday.

When he was on the pitch, he saw things more quickly than I did, and he often came over to talk tactics with me in the bus on the way to or from matches. Suddenly he would interrupt his argument because something along the side of the road caught his attention, something I hadn't noticed at all. Mancini had the ability to look in different directions at the same time – both on the pitch and alongside it – and saw the world with tremendous curiosity.

He made great use of that keenness of vision as a player, in this sport where a player usually has the ball for a very short portion of a whole match. You need to do something shrewd when you get the ball. Ingenious players also know what to do before the ball reaches them. Moreover, their technical mastery allows them to devote a tenth of a second here and a tenth of a second there to scope out the pitch. They know that they can't control the ball with one touch and that in the next touch they can place the ball precisely where they want it. If a player doesn't have that mastery, he needs more time to gain control, thereby losing time that could have been used to predict the next step, the next pass, the next shot.

It's a matter of reading the play. Routine is important, so you can sense where a ball is going to land.

When I was coaching Sampdoria, the owner Paolo Mantovani always called me the day before a match, wondering whether Mancini would be playing. I finally asked the boss why he wanted to find out about Mancini. 'Then I'll be there watching,' he said. The team's other big star, Gianluca Vialli, eventually heard about this. He was furious and went to see the owner. 'Why do you only ask whether Mancini will be playing? Why don't you ask if I'm playing?' Mantovani replied instantly: 'Because you're a guy who just runs around scoring goals. What Mancini does, that's art. When he has the ball, you never know what he's going to do next.'

But they were both equally important to the team. Gianluca ran his butt off, and he certainly could score. Players who run the whole match are worth their weight in gold. That's still true today. It's easy to be a centre back if you know that the opponents never pass the ball behind you. But if you never know what your closest opponent is going to do – meet the ball or take off deep – you have to be able to make instant decisions. And that goes for all players: the faster you can make decisions, the better. In the same way, players like Vialli force their opponents to constantly make immediate decisions, and that increases the probability that they will be wrong, sooner or later.

The best players are the quick thinkers. Take players like Xavi and Iniesta at Barcelona and Spain. They're small men, men who didn't spend much time in the gym during their careers. But their opponents could never get hold of the ball. They were that skilful, played with one touch. They had everything figured out before they even got the ball.

When I was national team manager for England, we played Spain in a training match in Madrid. I had players like Frank Lampard, Paul Scholes, and Steven Gerrard. But when they were up against Xavi and Iniesta, they never got the damn ball. It was a regular clinic on their part. We lost 3–0, but it could just as well have been 5–0. Fortunately, it was just an exhibition match. A while after the final whistle, the former great Trevor Brooking came into the locker room. He was the director of the English Football Association, and when I spotted him I immediately thought he was going to make some snide remark. Even though he's seldom snide.

He said that he had played a great many matches in his career, that he had also been a coach and representative of the Association. 'But I've never in my life seen midfield play like what Xavi displayed today.'

If you encounter such good football players, it's virtually impossible to take the ball. We're talking about players that act like they have eyes in the back of their head. Zlatan Ibrahimovic was one. When he made his bicycle goal against England at Friends Arena, he knew exactly where his target was.

The greatest players are, just as Mantovani put it, artists.

———

My years in Genoa were turbulent, not least in private. Lina, who was now fully healthy and lived like any other girl, started attending the American school that Johan had first attended. He later started at a boarding school in Rome, at the age of fourteen. But things weren't rosy at home. Anki and my marriage was rickety for a long time, and we finally got divorced. I was working more and more, coming home later and later in the evening, but I had also met Graziella Mancinelli, who worked as a researcher at a laboratory. We saw each other more and more, and Anki found out about it. That was the final nail in the coffin. The divorce took a year. It was a heavy load, and it was nasty. In the end, she and the children moved back to Florence.

Sometimes, even as a football trainer, you feel lonely and you struggle with both professional and private problems. Often I haven't been able to speak, not even with my closest associates, about my private life. But Tord Grip is someone I have always been able to lean on. This is vital, not least because there's almost always someone close by who's itching to take your job as head trainer. Tord, on the other hand, thrives best when he's somewhere off in the background, busy tending, raking the manège.

In the middle of October 1993, Paolo Mantovani died. I was in my second season with the club, and he fell ill that autumn. I was able to visit him at the hospital and realised that he didn't have much time left.

The funeral was something extra special. The priest, a friend of ours, was a devoted Sampdoria supporter who used to stand in the bleachers with our scarf during matches. Some of the players carried in the coffin, followed by the family and the rest of the players. Outside the church a New Orleans jazz band was playing, and the funeral procession made its way through half of the city. Genoa stood still that day, but in a very noisy and grand way. The intensity grew as we proceeded. It was a fine farewell. That's how I'd like to be honoured when my time comes. It shouldn't be sad. There shouldn't be sorrowful speeches and a priest who doesn't understand football.

After my funeral, I want my ashes to be scattered in Lake Fryken. Then the ashes can flow into the River Norsälven. Then it's Lake Vänern, Göta Canal, the North Sea, the Atlantic. And on to the world.

CHAPTER 8

Lazio

It's a long way from Blackburn to Rome. In every way. After five years with Sampdoria, I felt it was time to move on. The role of 'the Beautiful Loser' didn't quite fit me.

I was contacted by the agent Athole Still, who represented the steel magnate Jack Walker, owner of Blackburn Rovers. The club had won the Premier League in 1995, and after two lesser seasons it longed to be back on top. That's where I entered the picture. I signed with Blackburn Rovers and wanted to have Roberto Mancini as my assistant trainer. But Jack Walker thought the old great was asking for too much money, and both Mancini and I were disappointed.

Then another man with financial resources and great self-confidence contacted me. It was Lazio's Sergio Cragnotti, who also owned the grocery chain

Cirio. He, too, wanted to win, wanted his club to climb. This was a huge opportunity for me, and I managed to tear up the contract with Blackburn, largely because I recommended Roy Hodgson, the man who once had meant so much to me and to Swedish football.

When I arrived at Lazio, Roma's light-blue local rival, their trophy case was virtually empty. The club had won Serie A in 1973–74, but that was it. In the late 1990s, Lazio had more supporters outside the city centre than inside. The stadium was far from full when they played at Stadio Olimpico, and they had finished fourth the season before I took over.

———

I've often heard that I have a cool temperament, because I didn't stand and scream for ninety minutes. That's what the other coaches who were big in Italy did. Like Giovanni Trapattoni. He was highly successful and important to Juventus. He never sat down for a second during matches. He was full of emotion and passion and started firing up his players as early as their Monday training session when there was a match the coming weekend, six days later. So it became: 'Mr Eriksson, he's not impassioned, he doesn't have his heart in the matches.' Many trainers who are the wildest along the sideline are mostly nervous, so there's probably a certain amount of play-acting involved. That's why it was wonderful to watch my former protégé Roberto Mancini when he coached the Italian national team in the European Championship in 2021. He was cold. Scandinavian ice-cold.

That's not what he was like as a player. He was constantly yelling at his colleagues or at the referee. He never questioned a result, but when his colleagues didn't do what they were supposed to, he'd be furious. He was ejected many times. For protesting – never for violent play.

When you come down to southern Europe as a coach – this goes for Portugal and Italy – you soon learn that people there are not nearly as angry as they seem to be. To generalise a bit, they also cry a lot. They are very emotional, and that's a beautiful thing, if you ask me. Regardless of whether it's about cars, how people dress, or interior decorating, style is paramount, both at home and in restaurants.

Religion also plays a major role in life, and in football. At Lazio, the day before a match when I was living in Formello, we ate dinner together, and before the food was served, a priest would arrive, often the same priest. He held a divine service and then stayed to have dinner with us. He sat there and laughed, spun yarns, and drank wine with the players. They said their confession to him, whether they had problems at home or whatever. I never went to confession, but I was invited to the Vatican, by Lazio's priest.

'Eriksson!' said Pope John Paul, and showed us around. We got to see just about everything. It was an incredible place. What riches! But it is indeed a strange job. Is it something to aspire to? Anybody who becomes Pope becomes a rock star, worshipped. But the life of a pope itself . . . seems a bit bo-o-oring.

———

During my second season with Lazio, the rules were changed further regarding foreign trainers, so I could bring in Tord Grip as my assistant trainer. That season, 1999–2000, we had players like the Chilean Marcelo Salas, Roberto Mancini, of course, the Argentinian Juan Sebastián Verón, and Diego Simeone, Fabrizio Ravanelli, the Czech Pavel Nedvěd, and the Serb Dejan Stanković. At Lazio, just as with most other teams, it was a matter of getting a bunch of super-individualists and global stars to act like precisely that – a team. Some stars find it difficult to go with the flow, to obey orders, to follow a certain tactic, or to wear the club's suits and training overalls as a uniform. If a star wakes up one day and feels that he doesn't give a damn, that's also a matter of concern for a team.

My role as a coach was to get everyone to understand my way of thinking, my solution for how to do things, how we would be playing. The next step was for them to actually be a part of the team and accept the tactics, the way of playing football. In a team there will be friction. That's how it was in the 1980s, how it was in the 1990s, and so it is today.

An example of this kind of friction was when Marcelo Salas did not accept being replaced in a match against Chelsea. When he left the pitch, he took off his shirt, and when he walked past me he said certain inappropriate words, half in Italian, half in Spanish. In that situation, I was ice-cold, I didn't respond to him. After the match I looked at him, but there was no point in talking, not there and then. I had the talk the next day, explained how he should comport himself. I made it clear that his role was to play football. Or sit on the bench, or even in the stand if I, as the trainer, decided. My assignment was to select the best possible team.

At the same time, it was important for me to have the players dare to tell me their thoughts. I was the

Svennis celebrating Lazio's victory over Milan in the Coppa Italia, 1998.

What are you most proud of and why?

The times I have succeeded in creating the feeling that a team is truly 'my' team, that we are striving towards the same goal. It was like that with IFK Göteborg, Benfica – and definitely Lazio. Actually also during my time as the national coach in England, even if a national team is different from club teams.

boss, they all knew that, but for that very reason there was no point in bawling and yelling. That's also why I wanted to create a good atmosphere in all of my teams, because it was perfectly clear that the player shouldn't be afraid of me, and if they had good ideas, they were welcome. Not even *I* know everything about football even though I'm their coach, their leader.

If you get the players to come up with their own ideas and suggestions, with thoughts of their own about how the team should play, then they will continue to think about football all hours of the day, and maybe how they themselves fit into the system. It's a matter of getting as many as possible involved.

———

It's true that the job of trainer is tenuous. We can be fired at any time, whenever the owner, the president, the person in charge, feels like it. But I think, and I've always felt, that we're paid for our work and for the insecurity that's built into the job. It's not a secret what the owner requires or wants you to succeed in doing.

It certainly happened that the owner and I had different opinions. At Lazio they had a leading goal-scorer and team captain, Beppe Signori. He was tremendously well liked. In many ways he was the king of Rome. But after a few months, I went to Sergio Cragnotti and said: 'Beppe Signori must go.'

Cragnotti explained that that was impossible, that they couldn't sell the club icon. What would the supporters say? He was a truly skilled football player, I said, but he was too negative, pessimistic. We were doing great this autumn, but he merely sighed and said: 'What Lazio always does is to play well up until Christmas and then everything goes to hell. It'll be like that this year.' Every day I heard that boring rigmarole.

After a few weeks, I started putting him on the bench and told him he couldn't just keep complaining. We actually didn't quarrel. I merely wanted to change his attitude. I finally got my will, though, and he was sold.

The next day we played a home match against Udinese and lost. Five thousand hopping-mad Romans showed up at Monday's training session. They formed large groups and pounded the roof of my car. They were mad at me, disappointed because I had sold Beppe Signori. But then things turned around. We started to win again, and there was a new mood throughout the team. Especially when we added players with positive winner mentalities, like the Serb Siniša Mihajlović and Roberto Mancini.

I can still feel what it was like to stand down there by the sideline at Stadio Olimpico during a derby with 74,000 spectators. When the entire stadium vibrated with feelings, with songs, with nervousness, from energy, from firecrackers. I also remember how I couldn't wind down after a match, something I never learned, even though I had become better at relaxing in most other situations. I would always start planning the coming week, the training, and the next match, despite the fact that the referee had hardly blown the final whistle yet.

———

As a trainer, as a manager, it was a daily occurrence that agents contacted you. And agents are even more common today. They exercise great power over football now. When I had been with Lazio for a year, an agent got in touch. The striker Christian Vieri was interested in coming to Lazio. He was then with Atlético Madrid, his seventh club in as many seasons. I contacted him myself and asked if it was true that he wanted to come to Lazio. 'Absolutely. Sven, I'm coming right away,' he said. Then I spoke with Sergio Cragnotti, who immediately booked a meeting with three individuals from the

Madrid club. We met in Milan. It was Cragnotti, one of his sons, and myself. We finally started to talk business, and we asked: 'What does he cost, then?' We knew he had a contract. They brought out a figure, the highest transfer sum ever paid in football: €25 million. 'Sven, that's very expensive,' said Cragnotti. I replied that it was costly, to be sure, but that he was going to score a lot of goals. Then Atlético Madrid's representative suggested that they could imagine taking our players Pavel Nedvěd or Stanković, or both of them, in exchange. That was not on the table. Instead, Sergio Cragnotti said right out: 'Yeah, we'll purchase him for that sum.' From the time we started talking business, the deal was resolved in five minutes.

So Christian Vieri came to Lazio. He played the whole season, and he was as good as can be. He scored twelve goals in Serie A. We came second, and we won the Cupwinners' Cup. In the final in Birmingham against Mallorca, Vieri made the 1–0 goal.

The day he signed with us, he pledged that I would never have any problems with him. He was not smoking, not drinking and was training harder than anybody else. He only had one interest and that was women. Well, I said, who hasn't?

He drove a second-hand Mini, whereas the others drove a Mercedes or Porsche or whatever. His car was worn down and crummy, but he said he didn't want to put his money into some expensive car.

Once when he was playing for us we were on Sardinia, a place you go to if you have plenty of money. It's the same clientele that hangs out there in August that are seen at certain restaurants in Rome, and at the ski resort Cortina in the winter. They don't actually do anything. They just hang out together. Italians are superb at hanging out. They can sit and talk about nothing for any length of time.

The water on Sardinia is fantastic: you can see the bottom of the sea a hundred metres deep there. And the hotels are exorbitant. I was about to check into a hotel with Nancy Dell'Olio, who I was seeing at the time, and there was Christian Vieri at the reception desk, questioning and haggling about his bill. What they were bartering about was maybe 100 Swedish kronor.

After his first season with Lazio was over, he sought me out. 'I have an offer from Inter. I want to go there,' he said. Of course I tried to persuade him, came up with arguments like, after all, we're already a winning team and next season we are going to win the league. But he wanted to go to Inter. So I had to tell Cragnotti that Vieri, after just one year, wanted to leave and there was no point in trying to stop him.

So Vieri was bought and sold within a year. He had the highest price in the market both times. Cragnotti was a good negotiator. My advice – to double the sale price compared to what he was bought for – even I didn't believe in.

But Cragnotti afterwards said, 'I didn't demand twice as much, but nearly. And he accepted it right away. I should have listened to you.'

———

Another player from my time with Lazio was the Croat striker Alen Bokšić. He had played with both Marseille and Juventus, and had everything you want in a player. He was fast as hell, and huge, a Torbjörn Nilsson type. But it was hard to get him to pass the ball, to get rid of the ball. I was on his case often, telling him he must pass the ball, that he was too selfish. Then he said to me: 'Mr Eriksson, when I was young, I played left wing and I ran up and down the sideline and never got the ball. So now when I actually have the ball, I'll be damned if I'm going to give it up.'

Being a coach involves so much, like getting many personalities to fit together and form a larger entity. Not least, it's a matter of striving for balance in the team. In Lazio, for instance, we had a balance player in the midfield, the Argentinian Matias Almeyda. There was also Roberto Mancini and Almeyda's compatriot, Juan Sebastián Verón. I still felt I needed someone who could win the ball, who could play simply. So I acquired another Argentinian, Diego Simeone – and with him, we won everything. But he was a regular pig on the pitch. It was Simeone whose involvement with David Beckham led to Beckham being sent off in the 1998 World Cup. Very seldom were there problems with the players, but I remember one incident. Diego Simeone and Fernando Couto started to fight and I sent them off the pitch. They continued in the dressing room but the people present there – doctors and others – managed to separate them. It was strange for two super professionals to start a fight and I didn't know why, nobody knew. They both came to me the next day and said, 'It will never happen again', and it didn't. I still don't know what the fight was about.

Diego Simeone was tough as rocks and never smiled, and he's like that as a trainer as well. I've talked to him about his Atlético Madrid team. 'To play for Atlético Madrid you have to run your tail off,' he said. That was his simple philosophy as a player, too.

There's something beautiful about a philosophy like that, because I think a great deal of today's football unfortunately has very little entertainment value. Everybody's passing all the time. Players often pass backwards even when the opponents aren't quite organised yet. That's why I enjoy watching Pep Guardiola's Manchester City, where they actually want to move forward. If I were coaching a team today, I would play forward as soon as we got the ball. One or two touches, with plenty of deep runs. Always forward. I believe and hope football will get back to that.

In the spring of 2000, the newspapers were writing on a daily basis that I was going to be fired. Two draws and then scoreless matches against Reggina and Cagliari in January prompted the rumours during this, my third, season. But suddenly we started racking up key victories, in the Coppa Italia, in the league, and in the Champions League against Chelsea. We won our group, and that gave the whole team self-confidence. That saved my job. Sergio Cragnotti was satisfied.

But then we were eliminated in the quarter-final against Valencia, who finally got their revenge on me nearly twenty years after that UEFA Cup loss to IFK Göteborg. It felt as if our concentration dropped off in the matches – because a lot had to do with the league, where we won against Roma, against Juventus, against Venezia, Bologna, and Reggina. On 14 May we won the league – the scudetto – and could celebrate. That night 150 blue-and-whites partied till dawn, at Circo Massimo, and I was no longer seen as a beautiful loser.

———

Later that year, on the last day of October, I was presented at a press conference as England's new national team manager. But the idea was for me to remain with Lazio all season and not assume my new duties until 1 June 2001. The rumour about my move had spread rapidly, even ahead of the press conference. The players began to wonder, and the team captain, Alessandro Nesta, came to my office to ask if it was true. Yes, it was.

The English newspapers came to the training facility, Formello, which was surrounded by high walls. They installed cranes and had photographers sitting ten metres in the air. After the training sessions they asked the players questions when they were on their way home. The players got tired of that, of course.

The main goal for us in Lazio was to win the

Svennis with Roberto Mancini, 2000.

Champions League that season. But it was as if I had lost the trust of the players. And the supporters. They couldn't understand why I would leave them. I was a quitter. So one winter's day as I sat in my car on the way to Lazio's training, I realised that this wasn't working any more. I called Sergio Cragnotti and asked if he was on his way to Formello. He arrived there, and I told him what things were like. 'I understand, it's going to be what it's going to be,' he said.

The idea was for Roberto Mancini, my assistant

then, to take over. At least that was my idea. But he declined the job and went to the press even before I'd had my press conference. He really didn't want to have a discussion about whether he was the right person to take over. I don't know whether the club would have offered him the job. Instead, the legendary goalkeeper Dino Zoff took over as Lazio's new coach. He had been training the team before I came and had become an honorary president of sorts. He was being paid a salary for doing nothing, basically. Now and then he would come down to training sessions, and started to give me advice. After about six months he said: 'What the hell, Sven. You don't need any advice from me.'

The spring after I left, Lazio came third in the league, and the team was knocked out of the Champions League in the second group round. Even while I was still there, we managed to lose against Anderlecht away and against Leeds at home, despite the fact that we had acquired, among others, the Argentinian Hernán Crespo, and Stefano Fiore.

———

Sergio Cragnotti later wound up in prison, which I think had something to do with financial matters. I was very sad to hear about it. But I had already left Lazio. In our relations, he was easy to work with. He did what I asked him to do: he purchased players. That's the way it should have been in all the clubs I've been with.

With Lazio, I took over a top-level team, a top-level team that hadn't won anything. But if you looked at the roster of players, it was perfectly clear that the team should be a contender for league title. I didn't have a situation like that with Roma. They were too old, tired, and lazy. With Fiorentina, we weren't even close. Benfica was a major club, but they couldn't then, and can't now, compete with teams in the very greatest leagues.

As a coach, you always want the team to be even better. You turn to the owner, and, in the best of worlds, he listens to you and gives you what you want. During the 1980s and 1990s, the world's best football was played in Italy. Then it was the league that paid the most and the league where all players wanted to play. So, I finished while on top, you might say.

Even back then there were complaints about money in modern football. Salaries were too high, and it was time to put on the brakes regarding the millions flowing in. Around the turn of the millennium something had happened. TV rights began to cost much more. Suddenly football was on TV all weekend. Salaries soared – my own, just like the players' – and transfer sums sky-rocketed. Everything was going up.

And suddenly Roman Abramovich and oil money entered the picture. That was a new financial boost, and the football power-map was redrawn. Now England was the centre of the football world, and I landed right in the middle of that metamorphosis.

CHAPTER 9

England

In the 2000 European Championship, England had flopped, failing to advance from group play. Later that same year, after a loss to Germany in the World Cup qualification round, enough was enough, and the national team manager, Kevin Keegan, resigned, issuing the winged words: 'This is not for me. I'm leaving.'

I first came into contact with my agent, Athole Still, when he represented the capable English footballer John Barnes. Still turned up when I was coaching Roma and suggested that I acquire Barnes, although nothing came of it because, as I said, in those days Italian teams were only allowed to have two foreign players. John Barnes went to Liverpool instead and had a fabulous career, but the relationship between Athole Still and me continued. Even today, despite my career as a trainer having ended, he calls me now and then.

Athole began his career as a swimmer, and competed in the 1952 Olympics in Helsinki. Then he became an opera singer, with Opera Naples. Then he changed his job again and became an agent – both for opera singers and football players. A remarkable life: swimmer, opera singer, football agent. He does have a beautiful singing voice. Once Lennart Johansson, then chairman of UEFA, was visiting London, and Nancy and I, Tord Grip and Athole invited him to Les Ambassadeurs Club. Athole and Lennart started talking music, and Lennart mentioned that Frank Sinatra was his favourite singer. Athole countered that Frank Sinatra was his favourite as well, outside the world of opera. They started humming, and then singing, together. We were seated in a large dining room, and suddenly the room fell dead silent, and afterwards everyone rose to their feet and applauded. Lennart turned out to have a magical voice, and the two gentlemen sang with great authority and emotion.

Many years after the John Barnes story, when I was coaching Lazio, Athole called and jumped right to the heart of the matter: 'Are you interested in taking over England?'

He was the one who then brokered the deal with the Football Association, and I'm certain he received good compensation. It should also be added that without FA boss Adam Crozier, I would never have been given the job – as the first-ever foreign national team manager. The Scotsman was a businessman, a competitive lion, only thirty-five years old. He made his argument clear to the conservative forces in the Association that he wanted the best person for the job, regardless of nationality.

Crozier had his office on the top floor of the FA

Svennis and Tord Grip at the office in Soho Square, 2001.

building in Soho Square, and Tord and I shared an office on the second floor. Once, right at the beginning of our time in England, Crozier came down and knocked on our door. What the hell does he want, was our thought, assuming he was going to communicate some views about how we should do our job. But that's not who he was. He simply wanted to see how things were going and wondered if we needed any help with anything. He did this often, gliding around the office. He knew the names of all two hundred employees. 'Stop emailing each other all the time,' he would say. 'Go and talk face to face instead.' I liked Crozier, but he was probably too ambitious, because ultimately the old guard at the Association saw to it that he was fired.

When Athole came with his question, I had no doubt in my mind. My generation in Sweden had grown up with English football, with *Tips Extra* at 4 P.M., Saturdays. I would sit there glued to the screen, regardless of what crappy matches were being played on awful, muddy winter pitches. I actually believe that the average man in Sweden still knows more about English football than the premier division of the Swedish Football League. English football was what I was raised on, my school, and now I was suddenly going to be the national team manager. Despite my admiration for their brand of football, I wasn't quite sure what was expected of me. At any rate, outside of football.

———

As soon as I arrived in England, I started taking private lessons in English. The main thing was to learn all the football terms, but I soon discovered that you can't study your way to mastery of some things. Players like Jamie Carragher, Steven Gerrard, and Wayne Rooney – I never understood what they were saying. They spoke Scouse, the Liverpool dialect, a hotchpotch of Irish, Welsh, and the Lancashire dialect. 'Dammit, if you want to talk to me, you have to speak English,' I told them. But Wayne Rooney just laughed at me.

I did grow into my English, of course, but you're always a bit handicapped if you don't have full command of the language. And I'm not a natural student of languages either. I get along quite well in Italian, Spanish, English and Portuguese, but I've never reached a point where I understand everything. You can communicate with people, you can read the newspapers, you can watch TV and get by placing a restaurant order, you can get through training sessions, you can talk tactics – but then it's hard

How have your dreams and ambitions changed, if they have?

Throughout my coaching career, I have always dreamed of coaching an even better team. I have always been prepared to aim as high as possible, a challenge that has followed me throughout my career. All the way to the English national team, which was the biggest, the highest. But a national team is different from a club, there are longer gaps between matches and the major championships. I had left incredible popularity in Rome with Lazio's successes and ended up in England with everything that entailed. And, England is England . . .

Svennis meets the press after being appointed England manager.

to develop your language proficiency once you've mastered the basics. The main thing for me was to start thinking in English. If you think in Swedish, and have to translate back and forth, it takes too long, and the communication will suffer.

I don't believe the players' confidence in me as a coach has been impaired by me not speaking perfect English, Portuguese, or Italian. I don't actually think anyone cares about that or has judged me based on how I speak. In both Portugal and Italy, they were delighted that I tried, that I made the effort. There, people generally accepted my language deficits, to a greater extent than I experienced when I arrived in England. The reason I've never taken a coaching job in France is apparent to all.

My children, Johan and Lina, speak Italian, English and Spanish like natives. You can't tell that they're Swedish. But they got all that automatically when they were growing up abroad. You can't achieve that free-flowing command of a language when you learn it as an adult.

———

One of the first things I did as national manager was to call Bobby Robson, Kevin Keegan, and Terry

Venables, my three immediate predecessors. They were all very friendly, and they all had the same message: 'It's great of you to call, Sven. *Of course* we can get together and talk.' So, I visited Kevin Keegan in his home and had tea and scones. I received lots of encouragement ahead of what was coming and was privy to his own experiences, but I got only one concrete piece of advice: 'Move to Paris!' That way I would be able to avoid all the paparazzi. In London I would never be able to lead a normal life. I didn't follow his advice, but, given how things later turned out, I probably should have. During my five and a half years in England, my freedom was plainly restricted. I went to see a musical just once. Chaos reigned whenever I went anywhere in London.

Lina attended Norwich University during that period, and she never told her friends or teachers who her dad was. Once I visited her and suggested that we go out and shop for clothing. That was a major mistake. Instantly people began to gather outside the shops and point at me through the window. Soon the entire shop was packed with people, and I had to apologise to the staff. 'My daughter will be back on her own to shop. I'll come back and pay,' I said.

———

When I started, the Association wanted me to work together with two Englishmen, Peter Taylor and Steve McClaren. It was as if they felt they needed to be cautious at first. They maybe thought they would just be setting up cones and not have any say about anything. In those days, the training sessions were always open to the public for the first fifteen minutes, and then, when we were going to talk tactics and practise certain moves, the journalists would have to leave. That first session, I set up all the cones myself, and there was a hullabaloo. But I explained that I'd done it this way all my life and me becoming national manager of England didn't change a thing. I was in charge, even though Taylor and McClaren led the warm-up.

Many things in England were to be done as they always had been. It's telling that the English FA was the last association to eliminate the rule that the national manager must wear a suit and tie at all matches.

———

I took over England halfway into the qualification rounds for the 2002 World Cup, and in just my fourth competitive match, we had our way with the arch-rival, Germany. And on Germany's home pitch, no less. I'm still proud that we beat the Germans 5–1, that we allowed a quick goal but were able to come back, that Michael Owen scored three goals, that we played exactly as I had wanted us to play. That victory put the wind in my sails that every trainer dreams of.

Inspired by the win against Germany, two British comedians released the sing-along-friendly song 'Sven, Sven, Sven', which got to no. 7 in the British singles chart. I didn't have anything to do with the song, but it gave the accordion-playing Tord Grip the idea to get his friend Benny Andersson and the England team together and into the Top Ten. Tord and I were sitting in our office in Soho Square, and we shared a room. We didn't just talk about football, but also about music, about those songs that always get written ahead of the major championships, and I said to Tord: 'What if ABBA wrote our song? You know him well. Call Benny!' And Benny bought in right away: 'I'd be happy to, and I don't need to be paid a huge sum. This is a great honour!'

I talked to the chairman of the Association and with the board, and informed them that I had something for them: 'ABBA has taken on the assignment of writing the song,' I said, exalted.

'No, you can't do that,' they responded.

'Why not? Björn Ulvaeus and Benny Andersson have virtually never written a song that didn't become a hit!'

The answer was that Björn and Benny were not Englishmen, that's why.

'Well, I'm not English either, but I work here,' I sighed, exasperated.

I still don't understand how they could say no to ABBA. The English have their principles, and this was clearly one of them. Any other time, saying no is not their best sport. Instead they say: 'Yes, that might be a good idea. Let's think about it.' At first this led to a certain amount of confusion. Tord and I are just the opposite, and it took a while for the people at the English FA to understand that we didn't beat around the bush. They even learned to appreciate it. We said yes or no, and that was that.

———

With Lazio, I had the world's best left foot on the team, Siniša Mihajlović. Before that, he was at Sampdoria when I started there and was rumoured to be a rather mediocre left wing. I retrained him to play centre back, and he became one of the world's best. His left foot was absolutely magical, and he could shoot fantastic corners, free kicks, and sweeping passes across the whole pitch. I brought him with me to Lazio, and he was highly successful there.

As national team manager for England, I had access to the world's best right foot, no doubt about it: David Beckham. That right foot came to save me more than once, starting with my first autumn as manager. We played Greece in the World Cup qualifiers on 6 October 2001, and we had to get at least one point to qualify for the World Cup in Japan and South Korea. If we lost, an elimination match awaited, and if we lost that, it would probably have been 'Bye, bye, Mr Eriksson.' In the 94th minute we got a free kick with the score 2–1 for Greece. Beckham had missed at least five or six free kicks in the match and seemed not to be in his best form. Teddy Sheringham stepped forward and said that he would take it instead, but Beckham simply told him to step aside: 'This one's mine!' Beckham's home arena, Old Trafford, was sold out, and he smashed it into the upper corner. The entire stadium erupted.

In the World Cup, we were drawn in the group that Swedish media dubbed 'the group of death', together with Sweden, Argentina, and Nigeria. During my time as team manager the same discussion and the same question came up again and again: How does it feel to play against your home country? Do I really want England to win? I played against Sweden four times, and I rooted for England, of course. I wasn't sitting on England's bench hoping that Sweden would beat us. But, to be sure, it was a bit special.

The first match in the World Cup ended with a diplomatic 1–1 draw. Then we beat Argentina 1–0 following a penalty kick by David Beckham. Then we finished the group with a scoreless match against Nigeria. We came in second in the group, after Sweden, which had managed a draw against Argentina in the final match.

In the last-sixteen match, we won over Denmark rather easily, after an early goal by Rio Ferdinand. Then it was 'thank you and goodbye' against Brazil, despite having had the lead on a goal by Michael Owen. It was a clearly acceptable outcome for my first championship as team manager. Brazil went on to win the whole championship, but the loss nevertheless spawned the eternal question: 'Why don't England win in world and European championships?'

As team manager, just as every English person does, I had to present an analysis. During my time at England, I had a lot to do with Richard Scudamore. He was the CEO of the Premier League, and is definitely one of the people who have been most instrumental in developing the league, in making it as popular and powerful throughout the world. I thought, and many others have borne me out, that the main reason Team England don't attain complete success in the major tournaments is that the players are too tired when the time comes around for championships in the summer, because there's no winter break in English football. In countries like Italy, Germany, and Spain, they take breaks of varying length over Christmas and New Year's Day. In England they do just the opposite: they ramp up the pace, playing at least two matches a week. This means that it's the only major country broadcasting football during a time when many others have time off. So no wonder the TV audience is huge. A break would help to make our players healthier and more eager for championship play, everybody agreed. But it made no difference. 'You're absolutely right, Sven,' said Scudamore, 'but I just happen to be the CEO of the Premier League. There's no chance you'll get a break in there. Whether England win or don't win as a result, I don't give a damn. I'm an Englishman, but I represent the Premier League.'

Those were powerful words, but ultimately he had to give in, after I had left as team manager. The pressure was too great. So now there's some let-up, a short break affecting one third of the players at a time. They get those five days off, and as a TV viewer you can nevertheless watch Premier League all the time. There are many, many other matches for the players anyway.

———

There's a lot of joking in England about how significant the job of team manager is, but it's only partly a joke. It's usually said that it's England's second most important job, that only the prime minister at 10 Downing Street has a more significant assignment. You're a person that people look up to and place their hopes with. This means you have enormous status and are met with open arms everywhere. But it also lands you right in the middle of big-time politics.

In the spring of 2000, two Britons were killed in connection with the semi-final in the UEFA Cup between Galatasaray and Leeds. This meant that no Turkish fans were welcome to attend the return match at Elland Road in Leeds. Three years later, when England played Turkey in the European Championship in another return match in Istanbul, English supporters were denied entry. That was Turkey's response to the British government and the English Football Association deciding that no supporters should be allowed to travel to Turkey, owing to the precarious security situation. It was politically sensitive, and I, among others, was used for public relations purposes. I took a lot of flak for that in Turkey, that England's coach was talking politics, saying that no supporters should go because it might be dangerous. For many years after that, I've had Turks on my case about it. In the talk ahead of the match, Haluk Ulusoy, who was then chairman of the Turkish Football Federation, said that I wanted to stop the English fans because I didn't want them to witness a loss. He also felt I should be fired after the match, because I had no credibility left, and that I was only good enough to coach the national team of Patagonia.

I tried to calm the Turkish press, explaining that it wasn't my intention to offend them. I didn't want to be used as a spokesman, but that's how it turned out, and I should have refused to be a part of it. The match ended o–o, and that was probably just as well.

One person I had a lot to do with as team manager was David Dein. He was a great fellow, and was Arsenal's vice chairman for nearly twenty-five years. Among other things, he recruited Arsene Wenger as trainer. Today David Dein travels around prisons in Britain as part of the Twinning Project, where he links up football clubs with prisoner rehabilitation. He tries to get the convicts to think better thoughts about life, in order to get back on the right track.

During my time as team manager, he was always in Arsenal's VIP room before matches. VIP rooms are important in England. They're like the club's display window, meant to present their best public face, so they're like five-star hotels, with champagne, waiters, and fine food. David Dein was always there, greeting people and chatting them up. 'Hello, Sven, how've you been doing?'

Once he introduced me to his friend Boris Johnson. I took one look at him and immediately reacted to his hairdo. He knew absolutely nothing about football, Boris. Zip! I believe it was the first football match he ever saw. What kind of idiot is this, I wondered. He behaved like a fool, as though all was not quite right upstairs. Just a few years later he became mayor of London and finally prime minister. But me, I disqualified him right off.

Boris Johnson and I may not share many features, but if there's any similarity between us, it's that we both caused a lot of commotion in the British Isles. Everything I did was blown up, every little move. But I don't think I did anything wrong. Of course, I did date women I wasn't married to, but that's something many men do. I wasn't married myself, so it actually wasn't a big deal. I was a grown man who met grown women who knew what they were doing. That's what I thought then, and that's what I think now.

But all hell broke loose.

———

When the tempests were at their worst over my being named national team manager, the English tabloids sent their spies all the way to Värmland. They invaded Sunne and Torsby. Among others, they looked up Bengt Berg, who now, more than twenty years later, is writing this book with me. He has always had a special sense of humour. The *Sun*'s reporter understood that Bengt and I were old pals and was delighted when he told him about our heroic days as track-and-field athletes. This journalist grew even more curious, perhaps surprisingly, when Bengt, who is a poet himself, touched on my youthful weakness for Tibetan poetry. The reaction in Britain was a mixture of wonder and doubt: was I, a sensitive young poetry-lover from the forests of Sweden, thick-skinned enough for the job as team manager?

They never understood that Bengt was just pulling their leg.

I would never have dreamt that there would be such an uproar about my so-called 'affairs' with women.

Svennis as England manager, celebrating after England midfielder Frank Lampard's goal in extra time at the Estádio da Luz in Lisbon, during the Euros quarter-final between Portugal and England, June 2004.

I was on every other front page. Most men in Britain read the newspaper from back to front, because there's often some scandal in sports, above all in football, and I could dominate both the front and back pages for several weeks. I was everywhere, and that wasn't where I should have been, considering my job. My mum saved many of the papers, but she didn't really say much about it. Once she scolded Sky News, however. They made their way in through the hedge at my house, camera and all. They came and knocked on the door, and Mum was home. She opened the door and bawled them out in her pure Värmländian dialect. Newspapers had people in the bushes everywhere, all the time.

Once Dad decided to play a prank on them. He took some filled trash bags and put them in the rear seat of the car. He hid them under a blanket, so they'd suspect it was me, or something else of value in their world of rumours, lying there, concealed. Then he drove away, and when he left the yard, four cars followed him. He parked at the dump and, to the dismay of the journalists, took the trash out of the rear seat.

'Are you all crazy?' he said, when the journalists and photographers apologised.

Dad was satisfied, so he drove home.

———

It's hard to forget bad matches. They seem unfortunately to be etched into your memory more permanently than good matches, the good moments. Most people involved in football would probably agree. That's why I have a crystal clear memory of our loss to Northern Ireland on 7 September 2005. It was a World Cup qualifier, and we flew home right after the match at Windsor Park in Belfast, because the players had to get back to their club teams.

When I woke up the next morning at my terraced house in London, there was a dreadful din outside. At least fifty journalists and photographers were roosting out there. I had a chauffeur who drove me around, and when we left the house I was bombarded with the question, over and over again: 'Are you resigning today – or tomorrow?'

Our play was atrocious in that match, which was one of those matches that an English national team simply cannot lose – not against Northern Ireland. Everything was worthless. Wayne Rooney was worthless, David Beckham was worthless. It was windy and raining, everything was crap. I made changes at the half, but nothing got any better. Nevertheless, we did win our group, ahead of Poland, and we didn't lose any more matches.

As national manager of England you don't have many matches in store to salvage the situation if it starts going off the rails. The football press are usually knowledgeable, and not as bloodthirsty as the scandal press, but if you lose to Northern Ireland, they aren't kind.

Despite the fiasco, the Association gave me their full backing. 'Let's forget about what happened yesterday – nothing to worry about. We've won every qualifying match and beaten Germany away. This time it went south. It was a new low, but we're not going to talk about that match any more. Instead, we're going to concentrate on the next one,' they said to me.

That backing gave me the courage to face the press, even though I was both surprised and angered by the questions they asked. They even questioned my morals. 'After all, it's England you're coaching. Have you no shame?'

'I'm not resigning,' I repeated as a mantra, and leaned on words of wisdom I'd received from Tord Grip long before: 'If you lose a match, make sure you only lose once. Don't lose the press conference as well. Let them throw crap at you. Just don't answer.'

———

During the final phase of my relationship with Nancy, my life was far from peace and quiet. Officially we lived together in London, but the truth was that I had moved out and kept up appearances by occasionally living in our shared flat. For starters, I had met a woman on the side, and rumours started spreading. I felt I needed to talk with Tord about the situation. It was just before the 2002 World Cup, and everything Team England and I did was frenetically covered by the press. Ulrika Jonsson was well known in England then, a Swedish lass who had first appeared on ITV's morning programme as the weather lady. I was aware that it would be disastrous if this news got out, and that the Association would certainly want to have a say about it. I told Tord that I had met another woman.

'It's nothing serious really, but—' I started.

Tord said right away that he already knew about the affair.

'If this gets out, what do you think the Association will say?' I asked.

'Nothing,' he responded, adding that he had already spoken with them about the matter.

That was typical Tord Grip. He thinks about the consequences. He stays one step ahead. The Football Association didn't care about my private life, Adam Crozier had told Tord. Right after we had finished speaking, Crozier called. He had been in touch with a media expert who knew how to handle a scandal like the one I would be facing. That expert then contacted me, introduced himself, and told me he knew everybody in the press. He said he'd prefer to have nipped it in the bud, but there was no chance of that happening now. I was too well known, too famous, and Ulrika too. Exactly what the press loved. 'They'd like to have a case like this once a month, so we'll just let this one peter out,' was his recommendation.

It did ebb away after a while, but it was rough while it lasted, of course. Then a new tide came in.

———

The paparazzi never got any pictures of me and Faria Alam. I was extremely careful: we never met at her place or mine. But the press started to dig, contacting her friends. Someone knew, someone tattled. I suspected it was Faria herself, and I felt betrayed and angry.

I had been away from Sweden for a long time – twenty years – and had a good relationship with the Swedish evening press. They had my phone number, and when they called, I answered. But when this thing with Faria Alam, who was a secretary at the FA, got out, just a short time before the 2004 UEFA Euro in

Svennis and David Beckham, Portugal vs England,
Euros 2004.

What are your thoughts on regret?

A penalty shootout can become an unpleasant drama. This can be confirmed if you study the statistics of the English national team. Not least, Beckham's unfortunate feat from the 2004 European Championship when I was the national coach. Looking back, I regret that we did not bring in psychological expertise to address the players' nerves in pressured situations. A penalty shootout is an extreme mental situation.

Portugal, they stopped calling. They simply copied the English scandal press, where the *News of the World* and the *Sun* were the most active players.

So, when journalists from *Aftonbladet* and *Expressen* called to talk football, I simply said: 'I know you're not the one responsible, but you can tell your newspaper that I'm not talking with it any more.' When it was about football, they always called to check whether something was true or not and wanted to know what I thought about it. But suddenly the newspapers didn't care whether there was any truth to the rumours. So I didn't speak with the Swedish evening papers for several years.

It was true that I had met with both Ulrika Jonsson and Faria Alam on various occasions. But there was so much more that they didn't get. And the story had the added spice of the then-CEO of the FA, Mark Palios, also having had an affair with Faria, which the *News of the World* and the *Sun* also wrote about.

When Faria and I were together at a hotel, her boss, David Davies, called me and said: 'It'll be out tomorrow that you and Faria are having an affair. What do you have to say about that?'

'Nothing,' was my reply.

When rumours started flying about Faria also having had an affair with Mark Palios, the FA press officer, Colin Gibson, came to see me and said this problem could be resolved if I granted the *News of the World* a personal interview in which I talked about my relationship with Faria. Palios's name, on the other hand, would not be mentioned. I was to be sacrificed to save his skin. I told Colin Gibson that he was a son of a bitch and that I'd always thought so. He knew that – we never hit it off. Ultimately, both Gibson and Palios had to leave their jobs: Gibson because he had tried to obscure Mark Palios's role in the matter.

I've been asked many times whether I regret meeting Faria Alam and Ulrika Jonsson. Well, if I had known what it would lead to, I might have called it all off. But in purely ethical terms, I don't understand why, as team manager, I shouldn't be able to meet and have a relationship with whoever I want.

The beginning of the end for me as England team manager was when Athole Still and his attorney, Richard Des Voeux, received an inquiry. The idea was for the three of us to fly to Dubai to meet with a sheikh who was presented as vice-chairman of the National Football Federation there. It was a matter of developing football in the United Arab Emirates, and some kind of football school. That's how it was first presented. I would serve as an adviser.

We landed at the airport. No passports were necessary, as we were picked up in a limousine that stood waiting right outside the plane. We were there for two days, and I lived in a suite at the seven-star luxury hotel Burj Al Arab. The suite was huge, I'd never seen anything like it – as large as my whole house in Sweden. We had dinner with the sheikh and his entourage and didn't talk at all about what I thought the subject of conversation would be. Instead, they offered me a coaching job with a club that they hadn't yet purchased. They would also double whatever I earned as England team manager. I declined the offer, no matter how much money they were planning to dump on the table. I was team manager for England. This was in early 2006, and it was six months before the World Cup. They wondered if I would be interested in training Aston Villa. They also planned to buy that club, they said. But they expressed themselves extremely oddly, and one silly thing after another kept popping up in our conversation.

'If we fail miserably in the World Cup, we can talk about this. I'd probably be fired then,' I concluded.

The next day we were taken on a boat trip for some lazy hours in the sun. But when the boat

returned to the marina, the sheikh and his limousine had vanished, and the planned evening
meeting had been cancelled. The whole business
was strange, and the disappearing sheikh seemed
to be an enigma.

Until the resolution came in the form of
scandal headlines: 'SVEN'S DIRTY DEALS!', 'SVEN:
THE TAPES'. The *News of the World* – always that
newspaper – had rigged up the whole show. They
had paid for and directed the trip to fashion a lie.
The articles maintained that I could imagine leaving
my job as team manager to take over the Birmingham club Aston Villa, and for big money – José
Mourinho-size oil money – for my salary. When this
business with the Fake Sheikh, or Mazher Mahmood,
as the British journalist is actually named, came out in
the *News of the World*, Mark Palios's successor at the
FA, Brian Barwick, had had enough. He called me
up to his office and said that he was well aware that
it was the *News of the World* that ran Britain, not the
government.

'I didn't know that the *News of the World* was in
charge of the English Football Association as well,'
I replied. I made it perfectly clear that what they had
written was a pack of lies. 'You know I'm going to
sue them and that I will win,' I continued.

'I don't give a damn,' said Barwick. 'I like to sleep

How do you think your life would have been without football?

I can't even imagine that!

Svennis makes his way onto the pitch at half time of the international friendly match between Sweden and England at Ullevi Stadium in Gothenburg, Sweden, March 2004.

in on Sunday mornings. I don't want to sit for hours talking to the press about fake sheikhs and the devil and his maternal aunt. After the World Cup, we're done.'

———

One of the tabloid journalists was extra loud and animated at a press conference during the 2006 World Cup: 'If this is the way you plan on playing, we don't understand you. We don't understand how you think and why you do what you do.'

I sat at the podium and wondered how I should answer. Then I simply said what I was feeling, maybe for the first and only time during my stint as England team manager. I knew I was leaving after the World Cup, and I was so sick and disgusted with these damned newspapers and their journalists.

'It's only natural that you can't understand me. You work for and write for a shitty newspaper, and I don't think you understand football at all. I have taken coaching courses and worked in several different countries, so I'm not surprised that you don't understand me. You know nothing about this.'

The entire room cheered.

Afterwards I heard from British journalists that

they were surprised to hear something like this from me. They thought I had steamrolled the journalist. It's an unwritten rule that you shouldn't attack a journalist: No matter what you do, you should never have the last word. I'd learned that early in my career, that it only gets worse when you argue with a journalist and bawl him out.

———

In what would be my last championship as team manager for England, we were shown the door in the quarter-final against Portugal after penalty kicks. Frank Lampard, Steven Gerrard, and Jamie Carragher missed their shots. Carragher was sure-fire during training sessions; he nailed every penalty he shot. When it was his turn against Portugal, he looked confident. He placed the ball and – bam! – right in the goal. But the referee hadn't blown his whistle, so Carragher had to redo his penalty, and that time he missed. He was so experienced, and he still missed. It's so remarkable, what happened, and that tells us a great deal about the psychology of the penalty kick. He made a mistake that not even the juniors with Torsby IF make. Everybody knows that you place the ball, make sure it's not moving, and await the signal from the referee. Then you shoot.

I asked him later, about a year afterwards, what he was thinking. 'Blackout!' was all he said. His nerves had taken over, even though he appeared calm. It's clearly a game between you as a penalty kicker and the goalkeeper, but deep down your struggle is against yourself. How can you control your nerves? Your mental strength is paramount. So many great players have missed decisive penalty kicks in major tournaments and finals. In training, they score 99 out of 100 attempts, but suddenly they become a heap of nerves.

Research has shown that coaches shouldn't have their most inexperienced players shoot penalties, but neither should they ask their biggest stars to shoot them. The pressure on them is too great. You should have your 'grey' players, those who are neither the best nor the worst, take the penalties. They don't have the weight of the entire world's expectations on their shoulders, and they don't face the media guillotine the way the greatest stars do.

In the match against Portugal, it was instead Wayne Rooney who became the big scapegoat. He got a red card in the 61st minute of regulation, with the score 0–0. His teammate from Manchester United, Cristiano Ronaldo, went around bugging Rooney the whole time, and finally, in a messy situation, the

Englishman put his foot down on the crotch of Ricardo Carvalho. Rooney maintained afterwards that the decision was a mistake, and he was disappointed that Ronaldo had rushed up to the referee and tried to persuade him just before the red card went up. It seemed a clear and intended provocation from Ronaldo, knowing the temperament of Rooney, but these provocations happen and it's part of the game.

At the press conference after the match, I asked for the floor and directly addressed the journalists. 'Don't slaughter Rooney in your columns,' I said. 'He's young and inexperienced. And you're going to need him in future.' I suggested that they sacrifice me instead. 'You won't be needing me.'

Everyone knew that Wayne Rooney was easy to rile up. He was young and irascible, and he had great self-confidence. He believed he was already a world champion when he was seventeen years old. In February 2003, I selected him for the national team for the first time. He got to start in an exhibition match against Australia, and the day before the match I gave him the solemn message: 'Tomorrow is your debut!' He responded by shrugging his shoulders. It was perfectly clear to him that he would be playing. He wasn't at all nervous. Wayne was super-intelligent on the pitch, even though he might not have had that intelligence with him off the pitch. But as a player, he had a tremendous eye for the play, and one hell of a shot.

Much later, he and I were both involved in a charity match at Etihad Stadium in Manchester. The singer Robbie Williams and I were coaching the England team, and Harry Redknapp and the tennis coach Judy Murray were doing the same for a UNICEF team. Besides Wayne, the players included a number of legends such as Gary Neville, Paul Scholes, and Roberto Carlos, but also a number of female players, stars from other sports, and artists.

We pulled in some 150 million kronor, but it wasn't much of a football match. Which bothered Wayne no end. At the break he belted out in the locker room: 'Damn it, we've got to hold on to the ball! We can't give up the ball, because then we have to run ourselves to death.'

I didn't say anything, but I reflected that he hadn't learned a thing. The spectators had come to see the rappers and pop stars just as much as the football players. Nobody really cared, but the inveterate victory-minded Wayne Rooney was unable to take the match for what it was. At the same time, that's the same mindset that made him England's best goal-scorer ever.

—

We really thought we would reach the final in the 2006 World Cup. That's how good the England team were – should have made the final. I'm proud of what I did and proud of the team. We thought, and I still think today, that no other team was better than we were. And, as a matter of fact, Italy, who won the gold, weren't especially good either.

What could I say in the locker room after our loss to Portugal? It was my final match. Normally you can say: 'Shake it off, lads. We'll get them next time.' But we all knew that there wouldn't be a next time for me. There was a strange mood in the room.

The next day, before we boarded the bus to the airport to fly home to London, the new team manager gathered the whole staff. There were a lot of people there. 'A new epoque is starting today,' he said to everybody. 'And so I wish to thank you, Sven. I promise that you'll be invited, two years from now, to the final in the 2008 European Championship. You'll have a place of honour.' That was Steve McClaren's way of saying: 'I'm taking over now, and things will be better.' It was churlish of him, but that's what he said. Everybody reacted, including the players. Tord Grip always said about McClaren: 'What the hell, fire him.' As I've said, Tord is a good judge of character.

Some players just sat there, crying. On the flight home as well. It was not exactly a jovial ride. I know that Rio Ferdinand has said that the flight home was turbulent in many ways, that the plane was shaking and lurching, but I have no such memory. I do recall, however, that there was no singing, laughter, or joy.

When we landed, the place was crawling with journalists, but it was simply a matter of keeping a stiff upper lip. After all, I had been fired several months before the World Cup, because of the bluffing sheikh. It wasn't the best way to go, but in spite of the way it ended, English fans have always been incredibly friendly. I've never heard an unkind word about me, not at any of the many arenas I've been to.

I've never had any trouble with my self-confidence. In football, sometimes you're criticised and sometimes you're celebrated. It's never 'just right'. That's why you have to believe in yourself, and in the long run I've always known what I can do and what I can't do.

—

None of the 'scandals' I wound up involved in had anything to do with the football played by the eleven players I sent onto the pitch to represent England.

Nevertheless, it was the scandals that dominated my image and finally got me fired.

Athole Still and Richard Des Voeux had a meeting with the red-headed editor-in-chief of the *News of the World* after the incident with the fake sheikh. Athole had heard and knew that an article would be published on Sunday and told her that we would sue her. 'I don't give a damn,' she said. 'Sue us for whatever sum you want, take your place at the back of the queue!' Football journalists at least had the dignity to apologise when we met in connection with matches.

Later, I did sue the *News of the World* – and won. That newspaper, owned by Rupert Murdoch, ultimately had to shut down as a result of its way of pursuing journalism. It was not a closure that I mourned. They didn't give a damn whether what they published was true or not, although the main reason they went belly up was that they had made use of telephone bugging for several years. I was just one of their victims; also bugged were the royal family, actors, and politicians.

It was Scotland Yard that brought the information to me and told me I had been hacked for three years; my calls were listened to, and information about possible illnesses, erased voice messages, leaked bank accounts and much more was extracted, according to the police.

After the information from Scotland Yard, it took another two years before the *News of the World*'s culprits were sentenced and compensation was awarded. The money was given to charity.

I felt like a pile of shit. Here I had believed that Ulrika and Faria had tipped off the newspapers. I told the Scotland Yard agents that this explained just about everything, and they responded by telling me that everyone who had been victimised reacted the same way. No one could understand where the news items had come from. I personally grew suspicious of everyone around me. I even suspected my own brother. They had intruded into our most private business and then shouted it from the rooftops. They were emotionally dead individuals. This is what their bugging meant to me, as one of their victims, an uneasy feeling reminiscent of what you feel when your home has been burgled – you know that somebody has been poking around in your private sphere.

Since I was in England, there was a final battle royal with the media. Then all of us, players and leaders, parted, and went our separate ways. And I flew home to Torsby.

CHAPTER 10

Unemployed

Football is a poison, a highly addictive one. I've worked every season for forty years, apart from the time I left the manager's job at England, when I had a full year off. It didn't go well. I was stressed, nervous, restless. I felt physically miserable, distraught. That was when I realised what football means to me.

To me, football has always been number one. It still is. If there's a match I want to see, I'll watch it. I'm a goddamn egotist. Everyone around me knows that there's no point in introducing other plans. If Liverpool is playing, that comes first. Or if I want to drive to Degerfors or Karlstad to see a match, I'll drive there.

It's as if sports and football have killed off all other interests in my life. For one thing, unlike my brother and my dad, I'm all thumbs. When I was married to

Anki, we were driving along in our Renault and a tyre started to lose pressure. The car behind us overtook and held up a piece of paper with the writing: 'You have a flat tyre!' We pulled over, and I went and hid in the woods while Anki stood by the roadside to wave down some man to help her with the spare.

Literally overnight, I went from sitting on the bench for England in the World Cup, to sitting in a newly renovated Björkefors manor house, staring out over Lake Fryken. Nowadays I can enjoy that and find restfulness in the calm setting. I've definitely changed on that point. But at the time, I just couldn't stand the quietness and the dullness. I couldn't take it mentally.

Around that time was when Nancy and I finally ended our relationship. I didn't have any steady relations after the break-up, but I did meet a lot of women. It wasn't that these women functioned as consolation when I was feeling down, because what I was missing was not a relationship. It was football. I missed sitting on the bench, I missed being in the limelight, I missed the social aspects – and I missed the feeling of winning football matches.

My family, and maybe especially my children, maintain that I have no patience. They're no doubt right, but if you've spent your whole life leading others in a result-oriented activity, this is inevitable.

You need to get things done, and that means now, not tomorrow.

———

When I didn't have a coaching job, I longed for the social context that comes with leading a team. If there's one thing I've been good at, it's getting along with people. I've been good at getting a group to work together, getting them to accept what we've agreed on, and creating a good atmosphere. Of course, part of it is an inborn talent, but I also learned a lot from Tord Grip. He's phenomenal with people. But I've also carried with me my physical education teacher-training from GIH. We had a teacher at GIH who was extra careful to make sure that everyone felt at home, that no one was experiencing any fear or uncertainty. He got everybody on board, at the same time as he got us to do what we were supposed to do. That was inspiring.

It's important to remember that you can never create a good atmosphere on your own. You have to get people who are working with you to be on your side, and it's in this collaboration that that atmosphere is created. If you lose a football match, which is unavoidable now and then, the mood in the group can be the single most important way to bounce back. If you're experiencing bad vibes among the team members, things can fall apart after one, two, or three losses. Then it's a downward spiral.

But if you have a positive atmosphere, where everyone is working for each other and trusts each other, an atmosphere that leads to everybody in the group helping each other, the group will be strong, even in adversity.

———

Being part of a football team in Europe – whether it's as a trainer, a player, or in some other function – is to live an extremely humdrum life. You have a match on Saturday or Sunday, training Monday to Friday, and you have to be there an hour before training starts. As a trainer, that's more like two hours, which you devote to planning. As a player, you also have to get prepared, you have to eat, and do your rehab exercises if you have any minor or major injuries. After training, it's showers and massages for the players, followed by lunch for everybody. Then there might be a presentation and some new training, or the players can go home. When the weekend approaches, there's Friday-morning training and then travel after lunch, if it's an away match. Then everybody will be staying at the same hotel. And that's the way it is, even for major clubs, if they're playing a home match too. Everybody stays at a hotel in their hometown. It's fully accepted that this is the way it's done – the players can't simply go home. No one questions this.

But with Roma I tried to change this, thinking that everyone could sleep at home instead, and we could gather on matchday, three or four hours before kick-off, and eat lunch together. But the older players came and asked me if they could stay at a hotel the night before. They pointed out that they had small children and that their mothers-in-law were living with them, so they didn't want to go home. It was more fun to be away from home, or they just wanted to get a good night's sleep.

One of the things I miss the most about being a trainer, and that I missed during the year after England, is that very routineness in my life. In a way, it's simple to live a life where you know exactly what the day is going to look like.

Of course, it's also great to enjoy my newly acquired freedom sometimes. But I still want to have plans for the day. I don't have to sit here alone at Björkefors, I can go and see people, and they can come and see me. But I like to decide things myself, I want to be my own master, and, wherever I am, I like to end the day by reading for a half-hour, mostly non-fiction these days, preferably history.

I can miss that sense of freedom when I have people staying in the cabin at home. When my children come to visit, it's enjoyable and nice, but when the visit becomes a bit too lengthy, things get . . . I won't say boring, but I miss the solitude and freedom. That's when I can't do whatever I want to do, when I want.

But involuntary freedom – call it loneliness – is something I find awful. Not to be missed by anyone. Both Lennart 'Nacka' Skoglund and Gunnar Gren died alone, in their flats. That's sad, not least because things had turned around so much in their lives, from accolades in the limelight to the deepest loneliness. Of course, there's a whole gallery of football stars who lived their lives too hard and then couldn't adjust to life off the pitch. Paul Gascoigne, for one. He's still alive, but he has truly been fighting a hard battle with himself and his bad habits.

I can't say that I have an infinite number of friends. On the other hand, I know a great many people. I've been able to travel wherever I want all over the world, and there have always been individuals to meet at each destination. In a way, my thick personal phonebook has provided me with great liberty to live life on my own terms.

CHAPTER 11

Manchester City / Notts County

My first job after the lost year was with Manchester City. It turned out to be for just one season, even though we won both of the derby matches against United. It's an English tradition after a home match to invite the opponents' coach and staff to your office for a cup of tea or a gin and tonic. During these get-togethers, it's also an unwritten rule *not* to talk about the match you just played, about any referee calls, or whatever is gnawing at you. When we beat United at home 1–0, Ferguson simply came up, grumpy as hell, said a curt 'Hi!' and left. Then when we beat them again away, 2–1, he sent his assistant, Carlos Queiroz, who had to tell us a fable about Ferguson not having the time to come – he had to catch a flight. It was extremely unusual for a trainer not to show up, and really rude. I personally found those moments together extremely pleasant, regardless of how the match had gone.

We actually had a fantastic autumn. By Christmas, we were in a very good place in the standings, and with a team that had been thrown together, with several new players. It was all fine and dandy, and the supporters chanted my name from the grandstand. The club was owned by the Thai politician and former prime minister Thaksin Shinawatra. At the start of my time with the club, after a close loss to the top team, Arsenal, he said to me: 'Three matches ago, Sven was good. Two matches ago, Sven was good. One match ago, Sven was good. Today Sven was terribly bad.'

My assistant coach, Hasse Backe, understood what a temperamental person we were dealing with. 'This is not going to end well if we don't win every match,' he said.

Manchester City wasn't the same force in the world of football that they are today under the leadership of City Football Group, but I, along with Hasse Backe and Tord Grip, was nevertheless fired after the second half of the season was not quite as good as the first, and we came in ninth.

I received an offer from Benfica to return for a third sojourn with the club, but instead I made a bad

Manchester City supporters gather at the stadium to show their support for Svennis following reports that the club's owner wanted him replaced, May 2008.

decision and signed with Mexico as their national team manager instead. I never should have moved away from Europe, and I ought to have gone back to Benfica, but you make mistakes in life. I don't lose any sleep about this nowadays, but after a while in Mexico, everything seemed troublesome. A national team manager doesn't have nearly the same status as in Europe, where the manager is highly respected, and it's understood that he has the last word. That's not the way it is in Mexico.

The Mexican Football Association is completely

governed by the owners of the largest clubs. So, when I selected three players from one and the same club, the other club owners called to ask why I was being so unfair. Why hadn't their players been chosen? The national team was a display window, a way for the owners to be able to sell players and thereby make more money. They shouted and carried on. I wasn't prepared for that.

When seven World Cup qualifying matches remained, I was fired. But I wasn't all that surprised by the news after our 3–1 loss to Honduras. I had wanted to select two talented young players to play with the team ahead of that match, but I was called in to see the chairman of the Association, who told me that my team roster was not at all popular. The owners were constantly interfering. Money and politics determined everything.

However, my stay in Mexico wasn't a complete waste of time. After a merry evening at Mexico City bars, we were going to head home, my assistant trainer and I. Our bodyguard was also with us, of course. We walked out to the pavement, and two girls came up to us, and all I could see were the eyes of one of the girls. 'Aren't you the new national team manager?' she asked. She then pointed to a restaurant and said that she worked there.

Later on, Hasse Backe and I went to the restaurant.

It was a two-storey affair, and she was standing on the upper floor when she recognised me. That's how I met Yaniseth Alcides, from Panama, and that was it. We're still together, and she now lives with me at Björkefors, after many years of remote dating.

———

I've always been drawn to challenges. And that's a tendency that can take you places, both positive and, unfortunately, sometimes more on the shady side. The Nottingham club Notts County was precisely that – an appealing challenge. I firmly believed in what now sounds like a long, or short, if you will, cock-and-bull story.

Athole Still was still in the picture, and he contacted me again in the summer of 2009 with a new offer. 'There's a team in League Two in England that want you. The new owners are really keen on it.' But I told him thanks, but no thanks. I wasn't interested.

Athole, who is not known for his patience, called me over and over again. When I was travelling abroad, with a stop in London, he said: 'Sven, please. Can't you simply meet with them over a cup of coffee at a hotel since you're already in town?'

At the Dorchester Hotel I met two blokes,

Russell King and Nathan Willett. They worked for the offshore company Munto Finance, a subsidiary of Qadbak Investments, which in turn claimed to be backed by the royal family of Bahrain. In the background was another company, Swiss Commodity Holding, which claimed to have huge financial assets along with rights to all gold, iron ore and coal in North Korea. I didn't understand what I was going to have to do with Notts County, a League Two team, but I listened. The proposition sounded terrific.

The plan King presented was for me to come to Notts County on a five-year contract. My salary would be paid in corporate shares. He explained that their player budget was very large and that the goal was to reach the Premier League within five years, three divisions up. King said: 'Sven, come to us and you can do whatever you want. If you want to be the club's president, you will be. If you want to be sports director, you will be, and if you want to be the head trainer, you will be welcome. If you like to shine shoes, then do so. If you want to function as some kind of observer and see all of our matches, no problem. Your salary will be the same regardless. The club is more or less yours. We back you financially and won't otherwise be very involved.'

I was in my sixties, well aware that my career was in its second half, and I thought: 'One hell of a job.

Fantastic. I get a football club that's aiming to make it straight into the highest division, and I get to do whatever I want. I can employ anyone I want.'

Russell King and Nathan Willett impressed me with their enthusiasm. The club had already been purchased for £1, and everything was set. They had big plans for everything, from the arena to the training facility and the club's academy. They came across as open-hearted, generous, and knowledgeable. One of them knew everything about football, and the other was more interested in fast cars. King knew how to sell himself, to be persuasive – and to dupe others.

By the time a press conference had been called, rumours had already been swirling. The former national team manager was taking a position with Notts County. Nottingham was in a state of chaos. People went crazy. They cried, and they came up and hugged me. A new and triumphant era was at their doorstep, that was the sentiment that filled the humid air. The club is the world's oldest professional football club, formed on 28 November 1862, but it has long been overshadowed by its neighbour, Nottingham Forest. Now the black-and-white striped shirts were going to take over the football power in the town.

It was incredibly invigorating. Tord Grip and I were eager to exploit all the knowledge and experience we could muster to make this happen in the best way possible. The supporters suddenly had every reason to dream, to hope.

Tord and I moved to an elegant flat outside of Nottingham, at the expense of the club, on the River Trent. Nottingham is a fine city, and we lived in the same complex as Russell and Nathan. I was sports director and went to work every day. We saw every training session, every match. Every training session was worse than the last, sadly. A couple of days a week we had lunch with the two businessmen and talked about how we would develop the club.

With their help, I then made two major acquisitions: Kasper Schmeichel, who would play 43 matches in Notts County's goalkeeper shirt and later 100 caps for Denmark, and Sol Campbell, who had played centre back for England and Arsenal for many, many years.

The fever continued to rise. We were called a new Galacticos. Rumours spread that truly world-class players were on their way, like David Beckham, Luís Figo and Roberto Carlos.

Even though he had a four-year contract, Sol Campbell's stay turned out to last only 1 match and a total of 29 days. He was supposed to earn £40,000 per week. The experienced defender played against Morecambe away then asked our manager if he could spend two days in Newcastle. He got permission – it was Saturday evening, after the match – and then he called chairman Peter Trembling, who in turn called me the next morning to tell me that Campbell wanted to leave the club.

When the illustrious new acquisition Kasper Schmeichel was to make his debut, he invited his dad, the great goalkeeper Peter Schmeichel, and the whole family. There was a veritable delegation there from Denmark. It's customary in England to treat guests to a VIP lunch before matches, regardless of what division the club plays in. When I had installed the family in the VIP room, I went down to the locker room and asked the trainer, Ian McParland, to let me look at the roster for the match. Kasper, it appeared, would be warming the bench.

'No, you can't do that,' I said.

McParland stood his ground, saying he certainly could do that and telling me that the players had already been informed of the starting eleven. There was no way he was going to change anything.

There are few times in my life that I've been as angry as I was at that point. 'You could have told me that a few days ago. Now the entire Schmeichel family is here. If you don't change this by the next match, I can promise you here and now that you won't have a job here any longer.'

I then found Peter Schmeichel and told him

193

about the roster. It's a miracle that he didn't smash the restaurant to pieces. That's how angry he was. He screamed: 'You goddamn idiot!' He wanted to take his son home and swore a blue streak about what he considered a crap club.

'I can't go in and change that now,' I said in an attempt to calm him down. 'The trainer hadn't said anything about it to me. But I can guarantee that as long as Kasper is with this club, he will play every single match. Even if I have to fire the trainer about this.'

But it wasn't easy to calm down Peter Schmeichel.

It wasn't only the Kasper Schmeichel business, but ultimately I did have to fire Ian McParland. It's the only time I was ever on that side of such a decision. It was no fun. He, a four-square Scot, was furious. Russell, Nathan, Peter Trembling and I agreed first to elevate the second trainer, Dave Kevan, as a temporary solution, but as I was talking with Dave, McParland barged into my office, yelling that we had gone behind his back. He couldn't deal with being fired and simply lost his composure.

———

In late October, Hasse Backe came into the picture, as manager. He led the team in a draw against Shrewsbury

Town at home, and his last match was 12 December, when we lost 2–1 against Accrington Stanley, also in a home match at Meadow Lane. Around the same time, Backe got an offer from the New York Red Bulls, so he was gone.

Meanwhile, I negotiated with Roberto Mancini. He wanted to come to Notts County, even though it was a League Two team, and he was promised the same salary as he currently had with Inter. Right in the midst of these negotiations, I was asked to fly to . . . North Korea.

That's when the suspicions began. What was going on here? And Mancini was calling me every day then, asking us to send him a contract. He even flew to Nottingham. At the same time, Qadbak Investments were trying to purchase BMW's Formula One stall. BMW called me and asked: 'Do you think all this is on the level?'

'Well, I am starting to have my doubts,' I replied, honestly.

Nobody wanted to make deals with them. Everything was going straight to hell, and the question arose whether they'd ever had any money.

But in King's defence, although he doesn't deserve defending, when we flew to North Korea, a large group of other people came at the same time – geologists and mining experts, from Canada and South Africa. Russell King told me that I had to go to North Korea in order for him to be able to put together his deal. I was a member of FIFA's football committee, and North Korea had just qualified for the World Cup. One day when the others went off to look at some mine, I was picked up by a limousine, with a chauffeur and a bodyguard. I was shown around various sports arenas, fine facilities with plenty of marble. A North Korean official came up to me, and the female interpreter said: 'We need help . . .'

I thought they were going to beg for some football boots and footballs, so I told them that there shouldn't be any problem with that.

'We want to play in an easy group in the World Cup lottery,' the interpreter continued.

'That's what everybody wants,' I replied.

I stressed that I may be on the committee, but that I had no influence over the lottery. Not even Sepp Blatter, who was at the top of the hierarchy, could do anything about that. They didn't believe me.

'So, you don't want to help us?'

'Wanting to is one thing, but I'm not able to do so,' I said.

So, that was why I was there in North Korea, to arrange a good group and thereby good conditions for the North Korea team in the 2010 World Cup in South Africa.

We were in North Korea for about a week. During the visit, Russell King and Nathan Willett met, among others, Kim Jong-nam, leader Kim Jong-il's eldest son. I was at a meeting in the government palace, but I never saw either the father or the son. But the palace was unbelievably beautiful.

Then we visited a hog farm and saw the world's largest hog, who serviced all the sows there. I still don't know why we went to see this hog farm. Maybe it was to show us that they indeed had food. We drove on a motorway, and when we passed, people stood to attention but didn't look at the vehicle. In the capital city, on pillars of sorts, stood beautiful and well-trained ladies. They wore short-short skirts and held a red staff and a green staff in their hands. They used the staffs to direct traffic. These traffic directors stood at every intersection. The interpreter said they retired at the age of thirty-five.

On the trip home, the flight was delayed for several hours. The problem was that in those days if you flew to North Korea, you had to stop in Beijing, which was the only destination that offered direct flights. I told my hosts that I had a chauffeur waiting for me and wondered what I should tell him. 'Will I be arriving in London today?' was my question, and their reply was: 'You will arrive in London, I guarantee it. But I don't know how it will go for the others.'

It turned out that an oil consignment, some form of gift that was to be transported to North Korea from China, hadn't arrived. That was why the North Koreans didn't want to release Russell King. In Beijing, Athole Still and I took a plane to London. King was heading somewhere else. He walked with a crutch – he was born with polio – and when our plane from North Korea landed in Beijing, he ran off, limping.

'Are you in a hurry to catch your flight?' I called out.

'No, no, no, it's something else,' King answered.

He kept on running and didn't even say goodbye. I don't know what flight he was taking. Since that moment, neither I nor Peter Trembling have seen hide nor hair of either King or Willett.

Russell King later lived in Bahrain before being extradited to Jersey, where he was sentenced to six years in prison for fraud and larceny. By the way, on his trip to North Korea, he used the name 'L. Voldemort', as in Lord Voldemort, the great villain in the Harry Potter books.

Very odd gentleman.

I still don't understand why Munto would go in and purchase Notts County. Maybe they thought it would be beneficial for them to own an English football club. It worked in North Korea, at any rate. They rolled out the red carpets throughout our visit, and the government banged the big drums. The North Koreans received certificates showing that they had been granted purchase options in Swiss Commodity Holding that were worth roughly $2 billion. That meeting took place prior to the failed oil delivery.

If news of my visit had come out in England, all hell would have broken loose. 'You mustn't film me,' I kept saying, and tried to position myself behind the cameras. I knew a politician who firmly said to me before the trip: 'No, you cannot travel to North Korea.' But then I called the foreign ministry in Stockholm, and they had a completely different message. 'Absolutely. I'll make arrangements for lunch,' said the Swedish consul in North Korea.

When the bubble burst, Peter Trembling and I stood there, both employed by a football club with no money. We didn't have a penny to pay our players' salaries. Nor was there any possibility of our providing Notts County players with food. They expected both breakfast and lunch, but the club hadn't even paid its milk bill.

We travelled all over Europe to find a sponsor who could take over the club. We never found one, although we were close. We went to Norway to visit one of Norway's richest men, and he was interested, but we never reached a deal. Then the club was sold for £1 to a consortium led by Ray Trew, a semi-wealthy lad from Lincoln. We did it to save the club, right then and there, but it didn't work out either. He didn't have the money to invest.

Finally, the club had accumulated nearly £4 million of debt, and I was facing a dilemma. Time was of the essence, and I decided to submit my resignation letter, without demanding that Notts County should pay me the £2.5 million they owed me. I could have sued, but then the club wouldn't have survived, and I didn't want to go that far.

I worked there for six months. Tord did too. I never invested any money, but Tord and I thought we would receive shares worth great sums. We never saw any money, not a penny for all the work we put in. But I liked the club and the people of Nottingham. They were all heart and enthusiasm. Many of the players came to the club because they believed in me and the project. At my farewell press conference, I said that I felt bad about the supporters and the players.

Nowadays the club has Danish owners and is back in League Two after four years in the amateur, National League. But it's obvious that the whole business with Russell King harmed Notts County in the long run. When the smoke had cleared, I was regarded as having been tremendously naive to get involved in the goings-on. But what people don't know is that Athole Still and I carefully checked everything out, with the assistance of the national FA and the EFL, the organisation for League Two, and both came back with the same message: 'Go ahead! The money's there.'

I realised there were risks involved in the project, but, as I said, I do like an adventure.

CHAPTER 12

Ivory Coast / Leicester City

At the end of May 2010, with just over two months left before the World Cup in South Africa, it was finalised that I would be taking over the Ivory Coast national team. It was a fantastic assignment. I've never managed such a merry football team in my life. There was dancing and singing all day long, and yet the players were focused and disciplined. They gave their all, laughing the whole time.

Ahead of the World Cup, we were at a training camp in Switzerland, and when we were going to play the first training match, we travelled by bus from the hotel to the stadium. We arrived a bit more than an hour before the match was to start. It was me, Tord Grip, and my assistant, Benny Lennartsson. There were people everywhere. The whole locker room was packed with players, leaders, directors, and other important people. The only person who was not there was the equipment manager – with the shin-guards, shirts, boots, and all the other stuff.

Benny Lennartsson was furious. He said to me: 'Svennis, this won't do. We have to report this!' But I felt it wouldn't be right for me to start my assignment by arguing with everybody. That discussion would come after the match. Instead, we had a cup of coffee outside the arena, and after a long while, the equipment man arrived and plunked two big sacks onto the floor. The players threw themselves onto the sacks and started digging, yelling about their shirts and socks. It was sheer anarchy, and our right back didn't find his boots. He wouldn't be able to play.

I then decided that in future we couldn't have any directors or bosses in the locker room before matches. The World Cup was shimmering on the horizon, so we needed to proceed in some kind of orderly fashion.

The next day I talked to the team's big star and leader, Didier Drogba. I asked him how he and the others who played in the world's greatest clubs could accept the general lack of structure in the national team. He merely shrugged his shoulders and said, 'That's the way it is.' As he saw it, something special, something magic happened when they gathered to play in the national team. That magic was their strength, he said, their superpower, and the rules of the European clubs no longer applied.

And there certainly was something special that the players shared – they wouldn't let any problems bother them. They sang on their way to the match and on their way home. At our dinners the din was extremely loud. The person sitting at one end of the table would choose to talk to the person at the other end. It was also beautiful to see how they got along across religious boundaries, Christian and Muslim. To the players, it wasn't a problem. They were united by football, not religion.

I had only spent one day in Ivory Coast when I signed the contract, and then one day after that, so I didn't have much contact with the country itself. It was impossible not to be infected by their joyousness, but African football needs to improve its organisation. If that happens, then their finances will improve, to provide a stable foundation on which to build their success. As it is now, they often use domestic coaches during the qualifying period for championships. These coaches aren't paid very well, and provide a kind of low-budget alternative. Then they're dismissed and replaced by well-paid foreign trainers, who come in, as I did, for only a brief period. This strategy is untenable, of course.

—

Before the first match, I told Didier Drogba that we had a good chance: we could very well win the World Cup. I was certain we would reach the quarter-finals. That's how good the team was. But he just said: 'No, that's not going to happen. We can't concentrate in big matches, not for ninety minutes. Ultimately we will make fatal mistakes.'

Didier Drogba was right. We finished 0–0 against Portugal in the first match and then made two gigantic mistakes against Brazil, in a match we lost 1–3. We nevertheless made a decent World Cup appearance, but we were a bit unlucky to wind up in an extremely difficult group. The greatest disappointment was that Drogba injured his arm just a week before, so could never deliver the kind of play that would have taken us further.

In our final group match, we beat North Korea 3–0, the same national team that had asked me to 'arrange for an easy group' for them a few years earlier. They had faced Brazil in their first match and defended themselves as best they could, placing their

Svennis as head coach of Ivory Coast, speaking with striker Didier Drogba during the 2010 FIFA World Cup match between Ivory Coast and Portugal at Nelson Mandela Bay Stadium in Port Elizabeth, South Africa, June 2010.

own hope on counterattacks. Even though they lost 1–2, they achieved a sensational result. But in the next match against Portugal, they changed their tactics. Suddenly they went on the attack. Ronaldo ran the North Koreans ragged, and their trainer, Kim Jong-hun, was fired after the tournament. Rumour has it that he was sentenced to hard labour in a mine. The failure was regarded as a betrayal of Kim Jong Un.

In the group's second round, Portugal and Brazil faced off. Both teams would reach the last sixteen if they earned one point – and we would be sent home. Their match ended 0–0, and neither team made a single attempt at a goal. They were two teams passing the ball to each other in the middle of the pitch.

After our match against North Korea, the president of Ivory Coast, Laurent Gbagbo, came into the locker room. He embraced everyone and invited us all to a party back home. Gbagbo thought we had played good football but that the group was too difficult. In a way, it was a wonderful approach to losing and being sent home. In the bus to the airport, according to Didier Drogba, the players sang: '*Mister must stay four more years!*'

We had indeed been eliminated in World Cup group play, but back home in Ivory Coast everybody was ecstatic anyway. It seemed as if every single person in the country had followed our World

Cup adventure. We were celebrated on a large stage in a square in Abidjan, packed with people. Speech after speech was delivered, and when it was Didier Drogba's turn, the jubilation seemed never to end. 'You could be the president here whenever you wanted,' I said to him afterwards. He is still a hugely important symbol for the people of Ivory Coast.

I was asked to continue as national team manager, but at a lower salary. I declined the offer, quite simply because I was in need of money, and, moreover, I had seen the job as a short-term affair from the outset.

—

I once visited the football academy ASEC Mimosas in Ivory Coast, a place where young boys play football, attend school, and live. I was given a tour and saw the rooms where the boys sleep, with signs announcing: 'Didier Drogba slept here' – and over there 'Kolo Touré', and so on. The boys are only ten to twelve years old when they start.

Those boys clearly have a rough time, not least emotionally. They are living far away from their parents and have to look after themselves, in a sense. But they receive an education, and they get to do what they've been dreaming about. And at the next stage, if they're successful, they can become wealthy and change the lives of many people in their home country.

Over the years, African clubs have become better and better at training players, and this is indeed big business for the academies, who make good money selling players to Europe. These players are seventeen or eighteen years old when they leave, usually to some minor club, most often in France. If they're really good, they're acquired directly by the major European clubs.

The 2010 World Cup in South Africa was in many ways a great success for African football. There were drawbacks, of course, such as the massive security apparatus that impacted life there during those weeks. We weren't allowed to leave our hotel for anything other than training and matches. This was completely different from the major tournaments of the past, where you could live freely.

Many years ago, I stated that the time had come for an African country to win the World Cup, but unfortunately I don't think it's come any closer. The funding isn't in place, and the organisation is too flimsy, which is not unexpected, considering that the African continent is facing so many other challenges. In fact, African football has lagged behind in recent years not least because so many of their young players leave early to play in Europe.

———

After I had declined a continued assignment in Ivory Coast, I moved to England again, attracted by a new challenge. This time I became interested in Leicester and the Thai consortium behind it, Asian Football Investments (AFI), spearheaded by Vichai Srivaddhanaprabha of the King Power group. To me, Leicester was a similar investment to Notts County. We were to scramble upwards in the league system, and rapidly.

When I got to the club in October 2010, they were in a relegation spot in the Championship. Tord Grip was part of the coaching team, but this time more as a scout, with tentacles out in the world of players. We were getting better and better players, and when things were rolling at their best, the fans sang songs like '*When the Sven comes marching in*'. The team had a good winter and ended in tenth place that season. And then I had loads of money at my disposal, and we acquired players like Matt Mills and Jermaine Beckford, and were favourites for moving up to the

Premier League. The new season started out sluggishly for us, despite our acquisitions, and one year after I arrived, Leicester City and I agreed that it was time to go further.

I often reflect about this acquisitions thing, about how important it is to purchase the right players. The clubs I've been with that have been highly successful have been good at recruiting. I believe in trying to find players who possess the qualities of 'team player' and 'victory-minded'. Throughout my career I've been involved in many truly excellent acquisitions, but also many less successful ones, of course. Not least the players' way of being, their personalities, is something we should have checked out better in some cases.

Tragedy struck in 2018, when Vichai Srivaddhanaprabha died in a helicopter crash after lifting off from King Power Stadium in Leicester, only to come down in the car park outside. I remember him warmly. He was always there, at every training session and every match. He and his family, fine people, meant so much to the club, and the fact that I was terminated after about a year I understand. Things simply hadn't gone sufficiently well, and neither I nor the owner was satisfied with the investments we had made. It's a tough but wonderful business, football.

Since I left, the club has done extremely well.

Their winning the Premier League just a few years later was quite a feat, not least on the part of their trainer, Claudio Ranieri. I don't begrudge him for it. He's humble, loves his football, and I believe his players really like him.

On the other hand, underdog or not, Leicester City wouldn't have snatched the league title away from the giants if they hadn't had big money behind them, in their case from the King Power group.

CHAPTER 13

Dubai / China / Philippines

During my years as manager for England, I learned that the oil-producing countries in the Middle East have a somewhat different attitude towards money than we Värmlandians do. In London there are private clubs, members-only clubs, where you have to wear a suit and tie to enter. In these clubs, you can play roulette, one-armed bandits, blackjack, and much more. These are not gentlemen's clubs in the traditional sense, because businesswomen are welcome. If you're a member, then lunch is generally free of charge, and the clubs recoup the cost through their gambling operations. I was a member of such a club for five and a half years. After a year, I hadn't had to pay for lunch at all, even though I don't gamble. Finally I told the owner, a football fan, that I was going to pay for my food, otherwise I would stop coming to the place. He replied: 'At two o'clock this morning a man from the Arab world left this place. He was happy as hell. I'm telling you, Sven, that he had just lost £5 million. But he was just fine with that, and he's coming back this evening. And you're quibbling about paying for lunch . . . ?'

I never asked for the bill again.

I met Samir Khan in Dubai for the first time in 2004, and three years later he took over the management of my finances. He was sociable, a family man, and rather taciturn. He came to my office regularly, and I thought he was providing very good service. After about a year, however, I was warned that everything was not as it should be with him. But I didn't take that seriously. If I had, I could have salvaged a bundle of money.

I've only felt badly taken advantage of a few times in my life; Samir Khan was behind the worst one. He was entrusted with investing my money wisely, but instead he lost me roughly £8 million. It is, of course, hard to tell if he acted with purpose or just out of gross negligence and stupidity. But even the latter is at least close to a criminal act in my mind since he offered a professional service but lacked all experience and skill that was needed. He made me lose a fortune and almost forced me into bankruptcy.

I sued him and the case was settled. Though I got

an apology from him, I never got my money back. He was later pronounced bankrupt.

Basically, it was my own fault. I was too gullible, an easily duped Värmlandian. I was unlucky to some extent, but I was an absolute idiot to let him do whatever he wanted.

Samir Khan had purchased a house in Barbados in my name. Next he took out a loan with the house as security. I, personally, did not have a mortgage. Samir Khan thought we should borrow money against Björkefors as well, so he could invest it and get a good return, he assured me. I also owned a house in Portugal, and that, too, he wanted to borrow money against. That time I said no for some reason. I started wondering why it was so important for him to take out loans on all my properties. The thought was alien to me. I had never liked owing money to anybody. I only refused because of a gut feeling I had.

I felt dumb once I understood what had happened. My interest in money is nil. The same goes for contracts. There was no way I would sit down and read the fine print, in English. But I obviously should have. I should have employed someone who could help me. But I trusted Samir Khan.

My total lack of interest in money notwithstanding, I have an account in Switzerland. I checked up on it once last year. Before that, a long time ago, I had another account, also in Switzerland. It was overseen by a man I hadn't heard from for three or four years. One day, he called me. 'Svennis, I manage a lot of clients. Most of them call me at least once a week. The world is undergoing a financial crisis, with ups and downs, but I've never heard from you. Do you care at all how much money you have?' he wondered. He couldn't fathom that I had that attitude. But that's who I was, and that's who I am today.

Of course, I was deflated, sore and crabby when so much money vanished. It also affected my career choices, because I needed to bring in some money. Around that time, my house was for sale, and it really bothered me that it had come to this. But as I said to my son, Johan: 'We can only keep forging ahead and try and pull in that money again.'

It might sound simplistic and happy-go-lucky, but it wasn't in my genes to get depressed and destroyed by what happened. I don't think about it today. What good would that do?

———

Broke or not, I carried on out in the world. I almost went to China as early as 2011–12, but instead it turned out to be Thailand and BEC-Tero Sasana FC.

We came third in the league, and I stayed for a few months. It was a time of rumours and 'a miss is as good as a mile'. There was indeed talk of Ukraine's national team and of 1860 München, but instead I moved to Dubai and Al-Nasr. The club is run by Ahmed bin Saeed Al Maktoum, who owns, among other things, Emirates airline and the airports in Dubai, so there was sufficient money.

Once the owner and I flew to London, staying at a truly luxurious hotel there. We checked in, and then he said: 'I'll see you in the bar in fifteen minutes.' When I entered the bar, he and his friends were standing there in jeans and T-shirts. 'When we're out travelling like this, we're just regular. Moreover, nobody recognises us,' he said.

I had the title of sports director in Al-Nasr, and what I'm most satisfied with is that I reorganised their youth activities. For me, the main thing wasn't to winnow out the stars, but if we could find an A-team player, so much the better. The orders from above were crystal clear: we have to take care of the youth. Those in power in the country were scared to death that their young people might become druggies. No wealthy families sent their children to the football clubs, instead it was poor families, many of them immigrants with heavy manual jobs. One of the leaders in the youth activities was very careful to regularly look the players in the eye to see if they had taken drugs or drunk alcohol.

The A-team was trained by the former goalkeeper Walter Zenga, who played with Inter for many years before moving to Sampdoria when I was there. Even though we knew each other from before, it was hard to collaborate with him. He lived in constant fear and anger that I might possibly take his job. He felt threatened. 'Walter, I'm not here to take your job. I'm here to help you,' I assured him.

But that didn't work out. I quit, and he was fired. Lose–lose.

Dubai is a remarkable place, an artificial environment. Everything is fake in a way, a created reality built in the middle of a desert. Each building is larger and more stunning than the next one. And you can live as well as you like – if you have money.

You can obviously enjoy life, and I did. But it wasn't long before I wanted to get away. And there's also a downside: you can't freely express whatever you think or feel about the country and its government.

It goes without saying that I saw all of Al-Nasr's matches, attended by maybe a thousand sheikhs, all dressed exactly the same. There was no atmosphere at all, and I hardly ever saw a woman, even though women were allowed to attend football matches in Dubai.

The football itself was also bad. There were some

ageing former stars who had played at a relatively high level. But then there were those who were either halfway or completely washed up as football players. So I was tired of the football I saw during the half year that I lived there.

Now even more money has been poured into football in the oil countries, but I find it hard to understand someone like Cristiano Ronaldo, and what he's doing with his life there in Saudi Arabia. He plays for the club with the nearly identical name Al-Nassr. But I assume that he and his wife are living a very happy life. We never see him play in Europe any more, apart from his national team play. I can understand if you, as a player or a trainer, need money – I was in that situation myself. You sign a final contract to secure the finances of yourself and your family, but Ronaldo is still so good that he could play anywhere.

If sheikhs choose to invest their fortunes in football, sportswashing or not, then it's better, to my mind, to purchase clubs in Europe instead. For the truth is that nobody pays attention to the league in Saudi Arabia, and many of us football-lovers wonder: What joy is there in playing lousy football out in the desert, with few spectators in the stands and no atmosphere whatsoever?

Later that same year, 2013, I signed with the Chinese club Guangzhou R&F in Guangdong province, formerly known as Canton. I arrived there in the middle of the season and was attracted by the fact that it was in a league that was on its way up, and was filled with European players. I was given this chance, as I've realised since, because experience is highly respected in Chinese culture, and this benefited me and a trainer colleague, Marcello Lippi. By the way, I feel that the Swedish Football Federation should be better at, let's say, exploiting me and others with long careers in football behind them. I think it would have been advantageous, for example, in appointing the national team manager and other important posts. It's wasteful not to make use of our knowledge and our routine.

During my time with Guangzhou, I often had dinner with Lippi, who was coaching the other, somewhat better, team in the city. I, for one, social-ised largely with Europeans, and this of course had to do with the language situation. I had an interpreter who accompanied me to dinners, and sometimes we went out with other Chinese people in the club. They like their Chinese aquavit, and it was important to have it served with food, and there was a great deal of toasting throughout the evenings.

The extremely sports-interested mayor of Guang-zhou managed to have the Asian Championship hosted by his city, a competition covering many sports. He even wondered if he could help to train our team. Luckily, we averted this, but he did come to our training facility and play with his friends when we weren't training. I wouldn't say we became friends, but he was a pleasant man. The entire stadium had pictures of him plastered on the walls. One day when I came into the locker room, the gigantic picture of him that was usually hanging there was suddenly gone. It was as if he had never existed. Nobody wanted to talk about what had happened. But one of the interpreters said, after a lot of hushing and whispering, that the mayor had been accused of taking bribes during that very Asian Championship.

'We won't be seeing him again, ever,' the interpreter whispered.

Presumably the former mayor is alive but sitting under lock and key somewhere. I never heard anything about a trial.

———

In a way, I liked China. The club owners really wanted to win, to make their companies famous with the help of football. China wants to be best at everything, biggest in everything, so they obviously want to compete in football as well.

Guangzhou R&F had a youth academy. It was located a couple of hours outside the city, and it was fantastic to see the pitches and the buildings. It was primarily Chinese youths, of course, and then they had fifteen well-trained coaches from Real Madrid. But before I left the club, the owner fired all the Spanish trainers. He was dissatisfied and brought in fifteen Japanese trainers instead. He swapped out one football philosophy for another, and justified it by saying that he wanted discipline and order.

———

After a year and a half, I moved to Shanghai, to SIPG. I earned twice the salary I had at Guangzhou, and the team was really good.

The owner, a pal of the president, Xi Jinping's, was the director of the world's largest container port, the government-owned Shanghai International Port Group, hence the team name. Before he invested in the club, nobody – neither in Shanghai, China, nor Asia – knew what the abbreviation stood for. But just a year later, all of Asia knew what SIPG was.

For a few years, the government and other interested parties dumped money into Chinese football – in fact, far too much. Xi Jinping was tired of China being in 75th place in world rankings. The government announced that, as a first step, China would make it to the World Cup, and then they would win it. In many ways, it was the same view that the club owners embraced, but at a higher level. They've toned down this financial support now, not least in terms of salaries. They thought it would be a simple matter of pouring in funding – if you make the investment today, then the results will be seen by tomorrow. That was the reasoning, but that's not how football works.

I still believe in Chinese football, although it has lost much of the lustre it had before the pandemic. Now they're spending huge sums on youth activities, instead of on players and trainers.

———

When I was coaching Shanghai, we acquired Asamoah Gyan, an incredibly good player from Ghana. But he was injured and had a three-year contract. My feeling was that we were really stuck in the mud with that contract.

Then the owner comes up to me and says: 'How long is he going to be out?'

'The rest of the season, roughly,' I answered.

The owner thought that we should send him else-where immediately, but that wasn't possible under his three-year contract.

'To hell with that. Get rid of him.'

I then wondered what we should do about the money.

'Forget about it,' the owner said. 'I'll pay. He'll get two years' salary. Just get him out of here. We'll purchase a new player. Buy the best one you can get your hands on.'

I immediately thought of the Brazilian player Hulk, and suggested him to the owner. 'But he's expensive. Awfully expensive,' I added.

'Well, if he's the best, we'll take him. We're going to win. We're heading out in Asia and playing in the best cups.'

So Hulk came to us and became one of the world's best-paid football players. But after a few months, he and I had a quarrel. A big one. I ended up having the same problems with him as I had had with Zbigniew Boniek, who I tangled with when I was with Roma – I felt Hulk never showed himself to be a proper team player. Hulk didn't like me. I placed demands on him. 'You can't be like that. You have to play in a different way. You can't just dribble and dribble and then lose the ball and not give a damn about anything.'

It became more and more apparent that it was either him or me. And I lost. I had to leave after two, instead of three, years. Twice in my career, first with Zbigniew Boniek at Roma and then with Hulk, I have lost when I put everything on the line. And that's something I've done many times.

Key players are aware that they're the stars of the team. They're the ones who are supposed to lead the team forward, but that requires that I, as the trainer, get the team to function as precisely that, a team. If everybody, especially the big stars, play only for themselves, then I can't get the team onboard. I felt neither Boniek nor Hulk was able to make adjustments for the benefit of the team, and Hulk was closer to the club owner than I was. So it was thank you and goodbye.

The other players with SIPG did exactly what I told them to do, and they rapidly got better and better. There was very little promotion of stamina in our training sessions, but lots of football playing.

I thrived at the club and would have liked to have stayed longer if it hadn't been for the purchase of Hulk.

—

I've never been homesick, ever. Life has revolved around football, and I've been fortunate enough to experience the world, earn money, and lead a good life on the side. But there have been some exceptions, like in the Philippines, where I was not happy. Not by a long shot.

Accepting the offer to be national team manager there was the biggest mistake I've made, I believe, although I was always expecting it to be a short contract, a fleeting adventure. We played in two tournaments with me coaching. The first was the Southeast Asian tournament, the Suzuki Cup. We played well in it, even playing to a draw against Vietnam, who won the whole tournament. Playing in front of 40,000 spectators in the stands in Hanoi was a cool experience.

Then we were grandly eliminated after losses to South Korea, China, and Kyrgyzstan, who were all physically stronger than us. It was the first time the Philippines had qualified for the tournament. We simply parked our bus in the penalty zone and defended ourselves with everything we had. Playing destructively is not something I wanted to do, but we had no choice. We never got hold of the ball.

Nor had we been able to go to a training camp ahead of the championship. The federation couldn't afford it, and I was ready to leave at that point. But I gritted my teeth and forged onwards. I also felt bad about the players. If I had abandoned them then, they wouldn't have had anything left at all.

The reason I'd agreed to sign was that I was contacted by a German agent whom I knew, and he had had a lot of contact with Philippine football and the national team. They wanted me, whatever the price, so I figured it would be better to be there in the warmth than in Sweden that winter. I also hoped I would be able to have a greater impact than I did. I thought I'd be able to develop the team and the players, but I soon realised that the right conditions

Svennis as head coach of Shanghai SIPG FC, talking with forward Givanildo Vieira De Sousa during the AFC Champions League 2016 quarter-final, second leg, in Jeonju, South Korea, September 2016.

weren't in place. The players were upset and angry most of the time, and talked about going on strike. Many of them were older, largely washed up, and had had their football training in countries like England and Germany in their youth. Most had one parent from the Philippines and the other from another country.

It was wretched to coach the Philippine players, and there wasn't much interest among the populace either. We played home games at Rizal Memorial Stadium in Manila, and only a few thousand spectators showed up. Once when we were going to have a training session the evening before a match, we encountered a pitch-dark arena. The players suited up, and we stood there waiting for the pitch lighting to come on. Nothing happened. Then somebody showed up from the federation who promised to fix things. When he returned after a while, he said that the electricity bill hadn't been paid, so it would take at least an hour before the lighting came on. The players and I went home. After an hour the federation fellow called to say: 'Now you have lighting. You can train now!' But by then we were already sitting and eating our dinner.

We also had trouble with the buses we used. They were constantly breaking down. That's something that can happen, of course, but they used old, dilapidated buses over and over again. And the players never got any money from the federation. Instead, they had to pay out-of-pocket for the honour of playing with the national team. I only met the man who headed the federation once. Otherwise, we never saw a trace of him.

Then I contacted FIFA to get the Philippine Federation to start paying my back pay in instalments. It took several years and many series of contacts before they finally paid.

So, my final assignment as a national team trainer was also my worst.

———

It was never that I decided to retire after the Philippines. My door remained open all the time for new assignments, new adventures. The phone never stopped ringing, agents kept calling with job proposals. At the same time, I felt it had to be something sufficiently interesting, something with the right conditions. I didn't want to take a new job just for the sake of a job.

I enjoyed my life as a trainer, hanging out with the players and encouraging them, trying to teach them something. Also butting up against them once in a while, that's part of the job. Constantly having new principals or owners and flying around the world, those things suited me fine. The insecurity that's baked into the trainer profession was something positive for me. It's rather when I've felt secure that I've experienced anxiety.

About a year later, Covid swept the world, and the job in Jamaica that I'd been offered evaporated. It was a league in the Caribbean that was going to start up, with ten teams, and I was to be the trainer of one of them. But the pandemic made the sponsors reconsider their investments.

But, at the same time, I didn't want to leave football entirely. That's when Karlstad Fotboll entered the picture. I hadn't had an assignment with a Swedish club for more than forty years when I was presented as sports director in December 2022, after having had an advisory role for a short period. I truly believed, and believe, in the project and the people who are involved. The dream is still for Karlstad Fotboll to make its way up the series system, and for Värmlandian football to occupy a larger space on the map.

Sadly, it's a dream that will have to be realised without me.

CHAPTER 14

Björkefors

After England's exit from the World Cup in 2002, I spent the summer at home in Värmland. One evening, together with family and friends, I had booked the steamboat and tourist magnet S/S *Freja af Fryken* for a tour of Lake Fryken. As we glided through the water, I saw a beautiful white manor house and immediately felt: 'Wow, what a place!' We had just finished the first course of the dinner, and I asked the chairman of the Steamboat Association about the place. He related the history of Björkefors and mentioned in passing that the couple who owned it were having some trouble making ends meet.

The evening went on, and it should be said that we were not exactly sober. Tord Grip played his accordion just as the boat passed the house again. We pulled up to the landing, and I knocked on the door. The owner opened the door – it was the

Björkefors mansion.

middle of the night – and I said what I was thinking, that I wanted to buy the house. 'Don't you think this could wait until early tomorrow morning?' was his response.

I wanted to have somewhere to be in the summertime, when I was home from my training assignments abroad. I had lived with my parents, but now I wanted to find my own place, and I looked at houses along the shores of Upper Lake Fryken. I was close to buying several times, but fate had decided that I would become what is called a 'foundry proprietor' – the lord of the manor of Björkefors.

Nancy, my then partner, had a season ticket between London and Rome at that time, but she was with me the next day as we took a tour of Björkefors. We sat on the steps, and the sun was shining as we closed the deal. But the seller, an elderly lady, wanted me to continue to run some recreational activities there after we moved in. I told her that I would not, pointing out that she was of course free to accept another offer for the house instead. We shook hands, and the place I now call home became mine.

It was here at Björkefors, in the room on the upper floor that faces north, that the Nobel laureate Selma Lagerlöf is said to have written the last chapter of *Gösta Berlings saga* (*The Saga of Gösta Berling*) for the weekly magazine *Idun*'s competition. In Lagerlöf's topography of Fryken Valley, the manor was named Fors, and this is where the dastardly Sintram resided. That room is now my bathroom.

There was a lot of renovating to do: kitchen and bathroom, new floors everywhere, and, where the dining room had been, an outdoor patio with a roof. We installed big new windows that expanded the view of the lake and the hills on the other side. Many people close to me shook their heads with worry about the project. It was huge, and so much work. But I was obsessed: this is where I wanted to land. It

Svennis at Björkefors.

was my money and my decision, and I haven't regretted it. Of course, the repairs have cost more than I originally paid for the whole package, but it was all worth it. Every day I soak up the beautiful view of Upper Lake Fryken, with the prominent profile of Tossebergsklätten between the shimmer of the lake and the sunset in the west.

When I purchased Björkefors, I mentioned that I would also build a house for my parents. They appreciated the proposal, and that's what happened. Then Dad could work in the garden when he felt like it. It was perfect for him. But Mum died, and Dad said right away that he didn't want to live there any more. He needed something with more social life.

———

The world grew smaller during the pandemic. That was when I moved home to Värmland and to Björkefors in earnest. Now the entire area is my home. The career I've had, all the people I've met, have enabled me to socialise both with fancy people and ordinary people. It's incredible how quickly the brain switches. Like when I meet my old mates that I played football with in Torsby. It's nothing special for them, and the dialect is the same as it has always been.

'You want a beer, Svennis?'

Here I'm always the same person I was before, one of them, one of all of us with roots in Selma Lagerlöf Land. And with my feet on a football pitch.

CHAPTER 15

Modern Football

In the 2004 European Championship, my England was knocked out by Portugal in the quarter-final. We scored a goal in extra time – we thought. But the Swiss referee Urs Meier claimed that Sol Campbell was too rough with the goalkeeper, and maintained in interviews afterwards, over and over, that he would make the same call again. Urs Meier was sure of himself. What was acceptable in the Premier League was not necessarily tolerable in the European Championship. That was his reasoning.

A long time after, it came to my knowledge that Meier had had problems with the tabloids. I told him I was sorry for the intrusion into his life – I felt bad for him and told him I was sorry for that. He accepted my apology and thanked me. A human life and a person's health are clearly more important than a football match.

'I still think you made the wrong call,' I said to him, 'but these things happen.'

He was extremely grateful for our conversation, and to me this was further evidence that video-review systems like VAR were needed. Who would fans and the media attack then?

My being retired doesn't mean that I don't have any opinions about football. In Sweden there's a widespread notion among supporters and journalists to reject what is termed 'modern football'. To me, this makes no sense. As it is, Swedish football isn't keeping up with developments, and we're going to lag further and further behind if we do the opposite to the rest of the world.

There are drawbacks to VAR, of course, and there are negative aspects that I agree with the critics about. It sometimes takes time and can mess with the rhythm of the match, not least for the spectators. But it also guarantees that you'll have fewer mistakes involving the most important aspects: whether or not a goal was scored, if it's a penalty or not. The referee's view might have been obscured, some-thing else might have attracted his attention, and it's impossible for a ref to be certain about his call in all situations. Football is often an even sport: the margins are small. Sometimes the difference between the teams is negligible, a matter of chance, and then a goal makes a major difference. The main objective is for calls to be as correct as possible and therefore as fair as possible.

Moreover, if I were a referee, I'd love VAR. It removes a huge responsibility from refs, and players no longer protest VAR decisions. They've realised that it doesn't pay to rail against referees.

I was part of a group arranged by FIFA, a bunch of old players and trainers from all over the world. We gathered for a half day, and I submitted to Sepp Blatter, the FIFA chairman, and to Michel Platini, the top dog in UEFA, that we need to bring in goal umpires and a remote umpire, who stands on the line so he can see everything that happens in the penalty zone. The response was an 'Absolutely NOT', especially from Blatter. 'Football – even a World Cup final – must be refereed on the same terms as if you went out to Hyde Park, London, to play football.'

I told him he didn't know what he was talking about: 'In Hyde Park the match would be about, at most, who's going to pick up the tab at the pub. It's not a matter of deciding what's right and wrong regarding millions of dollars.'

But he was adamant, and Michel Platini didn't go against Blatter. He never did.

Those who resist VAR are simply being romantic

and nostalgic. That's how I see it. Of course, it will never be 100 per cent fair. Incorrect sending-offs and other decisions will always impact matches. But VAR is going to be further developed and become better and better.

———

In Sweden we've also had a widespread discussion about keeping the '51 per cent' rule, which means that private investors may own a maximum of 49 per cent of the shares in a Swedish club. As long as this is the rule, no major sponsor is going to want to invest any money – they wouldn't be allowed to take part in decisions.

There are reasons why the Swedish premier league, the Allsvenskan, is so damned bad. And it's getting worse and worse. The 51 per cent rule doesn't disrupt the wellbeing of the Swedish national team, but not many players from the Allsvenskan make the national team. The series and its players aren't good enough. To sit and watch bad football, as it's presented in the Allsvenskan, is awful, and it doesn't help that the series is unique in other ways. If we had more resources, we would be able to hold on to talented players longer. That would greatly improve the Allsvenskan. We have a great number of excellent football players out in Europe, not least offensive players.

Instead, Sweden fails, at home and abroad, in its defensive play, especially with centre backs. Football has developed into a game where you defend yourself in your opponents' penalty zone, whereas, in your own penalty zone, you build your offensive play. That development has occurred in the last ten years, and Pep Guardiola is one of the main people responsible for it. That wasn't the way things were done in the past: the ball simply had to be kept out of your penalty zone.

Now just about everybody, including in the Allsvenskan, plays a brand of football where you try to play yourself out of all situations, regardless of how technically skilled or unskilled the players are. The quality is too low. Instead, you hope that your opponents will move up so many players that spaces will open up behind the back line. It often happens that two backs in the penalty zone pass to each other, and it all ends with the goalkeeper, who should have the worst feet, sending off a long ball.

Sigh.

Selling players is important to all clubs in the Allsvenskan, and it's obvious that there's a connection between financial resources and success in sport.

Svennis.

What would you like your legacy to be?

That I always, in all situations, was myself. And that I in turn respected the players for who they were – I think that has left its mark on the football world even after I left the bench.

But, as it is now, our clubs, with the possible exception of Malmö FF, can't compete with, for instance, Belgian Division 2 clubs, when it comes to promising young players. No matter how romantic the clubs and their supporters may be, we'll never get a handle on Swedish football unless this changes.

Of course, there's always a built-in risk that owners will see the chance to haul in short-term profits, but that's where the Swedish Football Federation and Swedish Professional Football Leagues have a major responsibility. In England, purchasers must be approved by the FA and the EFL. We need a system like this, where everyone involved is vetted thoroughly.

I believe that a lot of good people would become involved in Swedish clubs, well-intentioned owners, if we changed the regulations.

—

It's true that owners do occasionally enter the scene who are not reliable. Thaksin Shinawatra is one such example. He owned Manchester City for a brief period, 2007–2008, when I was there. He paid the salaries, but beyond that he didn't have a clue about what we were up to. After one of the first matches,

Hasse Backe, who was there with me, ran up to me. 'Come here, Svennis, you've got to see something.' The players were warming down, chilling, on the pitch. They were running, slowly, and there stood Thaksin and his wife, awaiting the third half of the match. That was his level of football knowledge.

There are also lots of owners who have shown that they know what they're doing. Many people have opinions about Red Bull and their many clubs, and about City Football Group. But I don't believe that the energy-drink company or the sheikhs in the United Arab Emirates would invest in something they're not interested in. At the same time, clubs need money all over the world. It's an expensive business. Football is money.

There's a lot to be said about the oligarch Roman Abramovich, but he was a good owner, made sensible decisions, listened to people who knew what they were talking about, and thought about what was best for the club. But after almost twenty years, it all ended in March 2022. He sold Chelsea for about $5 billion after the United Kingdom and the EU instituted sanctions against him and many other oligarchs with ties to Vladimir Putin.

I've had quite a lot to do with him. He was about to purchase FC Dynamo Moscow, and at the same time I received an offer to take over as their trainer.

Then he changed his mind and purchased Chelsea instead. But first he called me to ask: 'Shall I buy Tottenham or Chelsea?' This was while I was England manager, and I countered with a question of my own: 'What's your objective?' He explained that he wanted to win, that he would win. 'In that case, you'd better buy Chelsea,' I said.

Before Russia's aggression against Ukraine, Roman Abramovich had a whole staff around him, and owned at least fifteen ships and yachts. Once, when he was in Oslo and I was home at Björkefors, I went there, to his yacht. He treated me to lunch, dressed in jeans and a T-shirt as usual, and he was sitting there watching a French league match. It turned out to be a match from two years earlier. He was zeroing in on a player he wanted to acquire.

But I have to say that he was a pleasant man, that I like him. He was so far from being overbearing and condescending. Early in his days as owner of Chelsea he or his assistant would call regularly. He invited me in for tea, and my chauffeur drove me there, to his flat in central London. You drove down into a garage and then took a lift up. The press never discovered that — that's how alert the paparazzi photographers were. I was there at least ten times, and he wanted advice about a lot of players. Such as Frank Lampard: 'Is he good enough?' Abramovich wondered.

The only time I asked him for any money was when I was supporting schools through the Shimon Peres Center for Peace and Innovation. We were helping about ten schools financially. His comment when I asked was: 'OK, because it's you!' The money would go to schools in Palestine, and Abramovich, who is Jewish, told me that there was no point in asking him again for money 'for Arabs', as he put it. It certainly is odd, but that's how it was. His view of that conflict was clear.

I had a lot of contact with the Portuguese José Mourinho during the same period. He had many of my players in Chelsea, including Frank Lampard and John Terry. Mourinho was always a paragon towards me. In our meetings and when we were in touch, he was completely normal, calm and collected. Once I sent him a message the day before I was to select a roster for a match. I'd heard rumours that Frank Lampard had taken a hit during training. Mourinho replied: 'Sven, when you pick a national team, those players belong to you. Together with your doctors, you decide if he can play or not. If he can, then I support you and the English national team.'

José Mourinho was actually the only trainer who answered me that way.

CHAPTER 16

Illness

Word of my cancer came suddenly and unexpectedly. I collapsed one day after jogging five kilometres, and the doctors could see that I had had a stroke, and that I also had cancer. The course of the illness could be slowed down, but no operation was possible. I was informed that my days were numbered. The day before, I had been perfectly healthy – at least I felt I was, at any rate. When I got the news, right smack in the face, I was hit by terrible anxiety, but since then, I believe, I've fooled my brain. It's very seldom that I think about death now. I don't sit here pondering what that will mean, what happens when it all ends.

I've always thought that it's a good idea to see the positive things in life, no matter how tough things get. I don't want to be that person who gets depressed and feels sorry for himself. Instead, I have tried to live life as usual, boosted by all the people I meet, both friends and people I've never met before.

Since I fell ill, since I found out that I'm dying, I've thought that it's largely a matter of carrying on as long as I can. But I've also thought a great deal about how I should deal with the illness in my outward relations. Should I say that it isn't anything special, that it's just the flu? Or should I mask how I feel? Or should I simply go out and say that this is the way it is?

As a public person, I wanted to avoid speculation, and I decided early on that the best solution would be just to tell the truth. At the same time, it was important to ask the media and others to respect the fact that my illness is something highly private, something that primarily concerns me and my family.

I finally made that decision in the car on the way to the radio station in Karlstad to record an instalment of the programme 'The Sunday Interview' with Martin Wicklin. That show turned out great, by the way. At that point, in January 2024, it had been nearly a year since I made my first and only public comment about my health: 'I, Sven-Göran Eriksson, have chosen to temporarily limit my public commitments, owing to problems with my health, which are now under investigation. I'm now focusing on my health, my family, and limited engagements with Karlstad Fotboll, etc.'

Only my attorney, Anders Runebjer, made a few cautious comments after that. What was known was that I was undergoing treatment.

Then the whole world knew.

———

I'm deeply moved when I think of all the greetings, all the fine words, and the love I've received during the spring and summer of 2024. I never could have dreamt that I would be able to travel to so many places, arenas and clubs that shaped me. To stand in the centre one last time. Every person should have such an opportunity to strengthen their self-confidence in the way that I've now had, pumping up my ego. In a way, we're all vain, so it's easy to confess that I've savoured all the celebrations.

When Robbie Fowler, one of Liverpool's very greatest stars, was planning for the charity match against Ajax at Anfield in March 2024 and invited me, I was radiantly happy. If I wanted to sit on the bench and coach the match, that would be fine, and if I wanted to sit with Liverpool's leadership in the stands, that, too, would be entirely up to me. It turned out to be a role as associate trainer to Kenny Dalglish. That's exactly what I wished for, a true Liverpool legend, both as a player and as a trainer.

I'd never met Jürgen Klopp before, but he showed enormous hospitality. I would have been able to use his office, train the A-team, if I wanted. He was joking, of course, but he and the club showed me so much warmth, such great respect.

———

I was completely surprised by what happened in Liverpool – and after that it's just gone on in the same way: Lisbon, Gothenburg, Rome, Genoa, Degerfors, Karlstad, Sunne, Torsby. Everywhere I've felt like a king, and these meetings have helped me to reflect about what I have actually achieved as a coach.

Hearing all these fine things while I'm still alive is a blessing, a gift. Not least, I'm delighted – and now you must allow me to boast – to be called unpretentious, humble, and analytical, but also that I speak the players' language and have managed to strike a balance between their various personalities and their ways of being, among all the stars. One of 'my' players, who I'm still in contact with, is Roberto Mancini, another is David Beckham, who was team captain, my right-hand man, during my years as England manager. Throughout the years since I left that job, we've met now and again, and we call each other with some regularity. When I got my diagnosis, he called a few days later and said: 'I'd like to come and visit you, if I may?' Of course he could. It then took a little while, but he arrived in his private plane at Karlstad Airport in early June 2024. We had an extremely good relationship during my time with England, and Beckham is Beckham. He's an incredibly fine person. He obviously didn't need to come and see me in Värmland, but I truly appreciated his visit. He brought with him his own chef – in fact he sent the chef to Värmland one day ahead. The meal was herring and potatoes and elk meat, following my wishes; it was an easy choice to make. We had one aquavit each. It was a highly relaxing moment.

Of course we talked about football, but we also covered much more during David's three-hour visit. What we said shall remain within us, and only us, as always between trainer and player.

———

I will never again train a football team. When I was younger, that insight scared me silly, but with time

Has your diagnosis changed anything at all about how you view the world, your relationships, yourself?

Every day is new, and I am grateful to be able to step into it.

Svennis is celebrated at IFK Göteborg home game against IFK Norrköping, 20 April 2024.

I've also learned to be idle. That's a skill I didn't have at the beginning of my career, but I did strive at least to switch off from my job at dinnertime – although it was hard for a trainer to set those limits. You're always responsible, so therefore you always have problems to mull over. 'Shall we do this, or shall we do that?' There's always something, major or minor, to ruminate about, and the solution to the problem won't be any better if you lie awake thinking half the night. The key is to be well organised and well planned. As boss, you're responsible not only for the players but also for your staff. That's why you're the one who makes the decisions, not only with the team's tactics but also when that group photo should be taken, when the sponsor should be visited. Then, if you're involved in every decision, you have to be available.

This is one of the topics I've taken up when I've lectured about leadership. I maintain that it must be awful to have a boss who isn't available. There are football coaches who don't talk with the players, but you have to remember that a football player is just like anyone else. He might be having trouble paying his bills, not because he doesn't have any money, but because he might not know who to turn to. You need to have somebody in the club who takes care of such things. It might involve trouble at home, arguments with his wife, children who are ill. Everyday problems. The same goes for the trainer, of course. There is a life outside of the arena and the training facility. Sometime you feel lonesome, with both professional and private problems. There are also things you can't talk to your colleagues about. But I've had the incredible good fortune, many times, to have Tord Grip.

He wasn't just my colleague and adviser, he was also, and is still, my close friend. He's one of the few people, I have to say, I can always rely on, who always supports me, who I can always turn to for advice, about virtually anything. It's a tremendous support to have someone you can lean on out in the big world of football, where there will always be someone maybe scheming to get your job.

Many times it has happened that my closest colleagues have been gunning to take my job. When I've asked them for advice, they haven't always told me the truth. But Tord is a person who would never reveal a secret to anyone. He would never ever have wanted my job, even if it had been given to him. We have similar backgrounds, and we share a view of football. Moreover, he knows football even better than I do.

When Anki and I and the children lived in Genoa, we were on the verge of divorce. She grew desperate and called Tord. And what did Tord do? He jumped on the first plane and flew down to Italy.

Tord arrived and was the family's counsellor, I'd say. But it turned out that there was no other way out. We did file for divorce. But it was good thinking on Anki's part to think of contacting Tord. She assumed, correctly, that Tord was a person I would listen to. It's a telling example of what Tord is like as a friend.

Tord has also done a lot of things for me that I either didn't have the time or didn't want to do. He's done it all without complaint. 'I'll take care of that so you won't have to think about it.' That's how Tord has always reasoned.

———

I'm grateful for all the love and all the support I've received, for all the letters, and actually for all the people who have shared their suggestions for beating my cancer. They all mean well, sending books, recommending what churches I should join.

It's also hard to find words to describe what I've felt during the spring and summer of 2024. It's wonderful, beautiful, fun, and my eyes have indeed teared up as I've stood in the middle of pitch after pitch and heard the applause and all the praise for my leadership and my way of being. I wish to be remembered as an honest person, as a good person, whatever that may be.

At the same time, I'm a bit awkward. I think: 'I can't be the one who . . .' It's probably a bit Swedish, Nordic, to have a hard time receiving praise in a relaxed way. I haven't been able to get used to that.

It's not easy to talk about the end coming. But I'm trying to be as realistic as I can acceptably be. I know what disease I have, and I know there's no cure. It can only be slowed down. I had to realise, when I received my diagnosis, that there's only one direction this can go.

I'm convinced that the earlier you accept your condition, the better it will be. It would be so easy to get bogged down in negative, bitter thoughts, but you need to combat those thoughts. Dispel them. Broadly speaking, I'm fairly good at that. It's true that dark thoughts do emerge as well, but obviously the struggle has been easier for me, with everyone having been so kind since I told them about my illness. Socialising with people is one way to head off darkness, exercising is another. And I read more now than in the past. Sometimes I long for evening to fall, so I'll be able to read my book.

And, as I see it, if you don't get a kick out of 60,000 people in the stands singing your name, then you will never get a kick. I'm very fortunate to have experienced this in so many places, and, with Bengt's help, to have been able to make this journey through time back to my life and my own career.

———

When my now-grown children, Lina and Johan, are visiting Björkefors, to be honest we don't spend much time talking about my illness. It slithers in once in a while, but it's not something we dwell on. 'Don't go around feeling sorry for me – let's live the way we always have,' I've said to them. And we do, as well as ever we can. And I still have my burning interest in watching football. You can always find positive things, great details, in any football match, regardless of level.

'Life is short, it's true, but if you live it right, it's plenty,' some wise person once said.

Consoling words indeed.

Conclusion:
King Eriksson's Royal Tour

Our closest major airport is Gardermoen on the other side of the border with Norway. The flight to Portugal takes four hours. It's 24 April 2024, and Svennis is undertaking his own 'Erik's Tour' or *Eriks-gata*. (Since medieval times, it has been customary for Swedish kings to visit various provinces of the country right after assuming the throne in order to consolidate their power.) Or should we say *Eriksson-gata*? After the invitation from his favourite English team, Liverpool, Benfica and Lisbon are next in turn. We're greeted and welcomed at the Humberto Delgado Airport, which is in the middle of the city, and are escorted to Hotel Corinthia, which will be our headquarters for the coming twenty-four hours. At the evening dinner, a couple of Svennis's old friends show up, and it becomes clear that they, including António 'Toni' Oliveira, have more than a lot to talk about.

The greatest of them all back in the 1980s was of course the legendary football player Eusébio, who left us ten years ago. But his favourite restaurant is still here, Seven Seas, and that's where we're sitting, with eagle-eyed attentive waiters around the oblong table.

The radiance from the Swedish football icon still spreads wide, whether it's in the breakfast room or on the street. And now, here we go again, time for another match in the mild April twilight at a sold-out Estádio da Luz. But before that Svennis is surprised by more than a score of former Benfica players from long ago, on the hotel's 24th floor, with a lovely view of the surrounding city.

At the stadium, Svennis is celebrated, and he allows himself to be delighted, he who once dreamt of blossoming as a football player, like Gunnar Nordahl, but instead now seems to be the Emperor of Portugallia v2.0.

Maybe it's his presence that helps Benfica win the first quarter-final of the UEFA Champions League, with 2–1 against Marseille, the team they beat many years ago in this place, and with Svennis on the bench.

—

Just over a week later, it's time for new Svennis celebrations at a match between the two blue-and-white IFK teams Göteborg and Norrköping in an Allsvensk contest at Old Ullevi in Gothenburg. Old, close friends are there: Glenn Strömberg and Glenn Hysén, Red Ruben, Thomas Wernerson, and many others.

As part of this event, Svennis must suffer through one of those interviews that start with his illness, and once again he manages to find a positive angle to the heavy thoughts. When asked whether he cries a lot, he answers: 'Yes, for joy!'

Just like in Liverpool.

It was here in Gothenburg that it all took off more than forty years ago, even though it was with another blue-and-white team, Torsby IF, that Sven-Göran Eriksson truly began his football career. And now he's standing here on an April day, allowing his feelings to condense into tears as he acknowledges the loving cheers of the Ullevi fans. Everyone remembers the formidable triumph in 1982, when the 'Angels' won the UEFA Cup. Now the situation is different, both for Svennis and for IFK Göteborg, who barely salvage a draw with Norrköping, largely owing to the eighteen-year-old goalkeeper Elis Bishesari, who blocks a penalty shot at the end of the match.

Behind him at Old Ullevi, Svennis leaves a newly christened grandstand that will bear his name for ever.

—

In the glorious month of May 2024, the passage from late spring to early summer is nearly imperceptible, and now everything is rushing ahead very quickly. The old brownish-grey grass gives way to the verdant green of the new. Up here in the High North people are experiencing a beatific feeling as the only reasonable response: it simply doesn't get any better than this! We need this, the sun-filled days and iridescent greenery against the dark colours of the ponderous spruce forest.

'Spring Fever in Torsby', declares the subheading of the advertising circular, and the centrefold presents Friday's programme: 'A festive day for the whole family in the centre of Torsby!' Courthouse Park abounds with families with children, which in itself represents a glimmer of hope for the depopulating municipality.

The highpoint of the day is of course the unanimous celebration of the football icon Sven-Göran Eriksson, who has now come to Torsby on his Erik's Tour. Svennis gets to ascend the stage, and once again confirms the importance of Torsby for his long and unique career. It's all about not making yourself greater than you are. Svennis says that it feels great, that it's a beautiful thing to be able to travel around Europe and be celebrated while you're still alive. He adds, once again, that he takes great pride in his background, in Torsby, in Värmland.

'I'm feeling good, and that's something we don't value enough when we're healthy, but that's what I'm doing now, when I wake up every morning overjoyed if I feel good. What happens in the future – well, that future's a bit shorter for me, I guess. But live your life here and now, that's what it's all about,' he says from the stage.

> 'The wings of dreams need grass under
>   their feet'
> Svennis – Stora Valla and Degerfors, return
>   ticket

That's my legend for Simon Klenell's statuette in honour of Svennis at the celebrations before the match between Degerfors and Utsikten on 1 June 2024. When we arrived at Stora Valla we were hardly out of the car before hugs were exchanged with old, former players with the red-and-white team that Svennis coached up from Division 3 to Division 2. His faithful companion Tord Grip was also there, decked out, in honour of the occasion, in a sun-blocking Panama hat. And once again Svennis praises his mentor when he takes the microphone out on the pitch in front of a jubilant crowd. With the arrival of the King Eriksson Tour at Degerfors, it can be said to have come full circle.

This is where his wonderful life's journey started.

All the events of the spring and summer seem to have provided him with the energy and strength that have contributed to his positive thinking, even in a difficult life situation, something that has engaged and inspired people throughout the world. And in Degerfors.

In Degerfors, Björneborg and Björneborg

Degerfors coming up soon
But I'm not headed to Degerfors.
But the train is actually
On its way to Degerfors
So I'll go along with going along.
Soon I, too, will be in Degerfors
Where people will get off and get on.
As I said, since I'm not headed to Degerfors
I won't bother to get off.
(Boarding doesn't apply to me
Because I'm already

On the train that will soon leave Degerfors.)
Life in Degerfors, just like the train,
Will go on as usual with and without,
    respectively, me.

We'll soon be in Björneborg
Where the train doesn't stop for getting off
    or on.
The train stops in Björneborg
To wait for another train to pass.
Björneborg has, or rather had,
Fine wrestling traditions,
But 'Björneborg March' has
Nothing to do with Björneborg,
At any rate not the Björneborg
Where the train is now standing (without
    stopping).
'Björneborg March' exists in my childhood
Inside a wind-up clock of brass
That radiated tinny East Bothnian military music
To a countryside lacking any wrestling traditions.

You have time to do some thinking in
    Björneborg,
Waiting for that train to pass. You can ponder
Whether the Degerfors brass band
With roots hundreds of years back, ever, often,
Or never played 'Björneborg March'.

269

Just as, somewhat nostalgically, you can bring
    to mind
Two of Degerfors' legendary goalkeepers:
Skjorta Bergström, who hung by his knees from
    the crossbar
And his successor, Sippa Tinglöf, famous
For his long throw-outs, a joy to remember.

Once, at a restaurant in Finland, in the city
    of Pori,
Which is called Björneborg in Swedish,
    something
Remarkable happened: One after another, more
    and more,
Soon everyone – except me – began to blow
    their different instruments,
On the stage, on chairs, on tables . . . And if you
    didn't have anything
To blow into, you had to grab bottles and
    glasses
In this marvellous cacophony.
The next day I saw on a poster
That PORI JAZZ was underway in the city.

Soon I'll be neither here nor there
But it's the same lovely spring rain
That falls in Degerfors, Björneborg
And Björneborg.

> That's the sort of thing
> That can be taken
> As a consolation.

For many of us, death is a scalding hot porridge that we tend to hover above. Even though death is the only certainty for everyone born into this earthly life, it is nevertheless an issue that's hard to deal with, and we prefer to avoid it. Svennis is far from unique in his fate – he, too, is going to pass away. But few people tackle their 'sentence' the way he is currently doing. He wants to savour every new day that awaits him when he opens his eyes after a night's sleep. 'Life exists as long as it lasts,' is his recipe, just as simple as it's useful. And in this, there's something important that we can all take in: Since nothing lasts for ever, it should be possible to live as if our days are numbered, even though we don't know what that grand total will be.

It's just before Midsummer 2024, and, as usual, Svennis has followed me out onto the steps as I'm heading home.

'Have you seen that I have a new flag?' he says in Värmlandian.

He points at the flagpole beyond the balustrade, and there hangs a full-size blue-and-yellow Swedish flag instead of the old streamer.

'I celebrate every day,' he says, 'that I'm alive!'

I sit behind the wheel and wave out the side window. Svennis waves back and looks up at the flag billowing in the June breeze.

———

During these mornings that Svennis and I have shared, we've slowly but surely penetrated each other's treasure troves, and wardrobes, of memories and experiences. We've played ping pong with our recollections, and we've returned to another era and reality. In our youth, the future lay as an infinitely large, blank sheet of paper before us, and no one could have imagined what narratives would play out there.

But now we know.

We've tried to convey these narratives as honestly and clearly as possible and with no thought of making headlines. Being Svennis's fellow traveller on this journey both backwards and forwards in time has been a dizzying adventure. The insight that so many people, of varying backgrounds and with shifting conditions, could find a home in the extended family that is called Football had never truly occurred to me. But precisely this – to create a green rectangle large enough for both dreams and drama and at the same time give people's differences free rein – can be seen as consoling and necessary in our conflict-filled times. Football rolls onward, and our conversations will also continue – as long as there's coffee left in the pot!

Svennis and Bengt, 2024.

Upwards / Downwards

These frantic men
Straining their neck tendons
To the breaking point.
Hanging in bunches
Over the grass; at night
They dream of paradise,
That they are giraffes who reach up
To the most delightful fruits.
But when they awaken
They see that they are
Simple football kickers
And they realise for good:
Vigour must come
From below.

Bengt Berg

Picture Credits

Andrew Yates, Stringer via Getty Images: p. 187

Bjorn Larsson Rosvall, TT News Agency via Alamy Stock Photo: p. 257

Courtesy of Jens Assur via TT News Agency: p. 244

Courtesy of Tommy Pedersen: p. 274

Grazia Neri, Stringer via Getty Images: p. 133

Image courtesy of IMAGO: p. 90

Lasse Jansson, Expressen, TT News Agency via Alamy Stock Photo: p. 65

Laurence Grififths via Getty Images: p. 169, 207

Martin Rose via Getty Images: p. 162

Power Sport Images via Getty Images: p. 229

Private archive / Public domain: pp. xii, xv

Private archive: pp. 2, 8, 12, 20

Professional Sport via Getty Images: p. 107

Sven-Erik Dahlstrom via Alamy Stock Photo: p. 16

Tommy Svensson, DN, TT News Agency via Alamy Stock Photo: p. 93

TT News Agency via Alamy Stock Photo: pp. 31, 33, 46, 50, 62, 74, 84, 122, 139, 143, 234, 236
Vincenzo Pinto via Getty Images: p. 156